General
X-Efficiency Theory
and Economic Development

ECONOMIC DEVELOPMENT SERIES

General Editor
Gerald M. Meier, Professor of International
Economics, Stanford University

Published
EMPLOYMENT, TECHNOLOGY, AND DEVELOPMENT
  Amartya Sen
AGRICULTURE AND STRUCTURAL TRANSFORMATIONS
  Bruce F. Johnston and Peter Kilby
HUMAN RESOURCES AS THE WEALTH OF NATIONS
  Frederick H. Harbison
FINANCIAL DEEPENING IN ECONOMIC DEVELOPMENT
  Edward S. Shaw
ECONOMIC THEORY AND UNDERDEVELOPED COUNTRIES
  H. Myint

General
X-Efficiency Theory
and Economic Development

HARVEY LEIBENSTEIN
Harvard University

New York
OXFORD UNIVERSITY PRESS
London 1978 Toronto

Copyright © 1978 by Oxford University Press, Inc.

Library of Congress Cataloging in Publication Data

Leibenstein, Harvey.
  General X-efficiency theory and economic
development.

  (Economic development series)
  Includes index.
  1. Economic development. I. Title. II. Ti-
tle: X-efficiency theory and economic development.
HD82.L342   338.9   77-16563
ISBN 0-19-502-379-X
ISBN 0-19-502-380-3 pbk.

Printed in the United States of America

Introduction to the Economic Development Series

Two centuries ago it all began with *The Wealth of Nations;* today it is called the Poverty of Nations. If economics has always been asked to propose means of social betterment, and if economists are, as Lord Keynes suggested, the trustees of the possibility of civilization—then the problems of world poverty will persistently challenge each generation of economists. But what is new for this generation is the concentrated effort by so many countries to undertake conscious programs of economic development. With the heightened awareness of world inequalities, development policies have been deliberately adopted on a national basis and supported by international institutions.

The time has come for a reappraisal of this experience. This Economic Development Series has therefore been designed to take a hard look at the central problems and strategic policy issues that have emerged to the forefront of development efforts. Recognizing that it has become impossible and undesirable for any one author to attempt to cover the entire subject of economic development, this series concentrates on a set of special problems analyzed by authors who are widely recognized authorities in their respective fields and who have had extensive experience in the developing countries. Each volume offers an incisive study of a specific problem area that now requires more understanding by students and practitioners of development alike. The treatment emphasizes both experience and theory. Taken together, the volumes in this Series formulate a number of policies that may be better designed to cope with some of the most troublesome problems of development.

G. M. MEIER

Preface

The view taken behind this work is that traditional microtheory represents an idealized case under which the economy works in an optimally efficient manner. Thus it represents a standard against which economic behavior can be judged, but it is not what really goes on in an economy. What I have referred to as general X-efficiency attempts to provide a more realistic framework within which the neoclassical idealized state is a special case. Since economic development is such a vast subject and indefinitely expansible, the applications of X-efficiency theory could be made only to some aspects of the problem. It is hoped that other areas that can usefully be analyzed on the basis of this framework will suggest themselves to readers.

While the final version of this book was written more or less continuously over the period of about eighteen months, some embryonic versions appeared earlier as contributions to symposia and as an article in the *Quarterly Journal of Economics*. For permission to use liberally portions of these published works I would like to thank the following:

The Macmillan Company, for permission to use portions of my essay "Efficiency Wages, X-Efficiency and Urban Unemployment," which appeared in *Economic Development and Planning*, edited by Willi Sellekaert.

Praeger Publishing Company, Division of Holt, Rinehart & Winston, for permission to use portions of my article "Notes on X-Efficiency and Technical Progress," which appeared in *Micro Aspects of Development,* edited by Eliezer B. Ayal.

John Wiley & Sons, Inc., for permission to use portions of my article "The Economic Theory of Fertility Decline," which appeared in the February 1975 issue of the *Quarterly Journal of Economics.*

Cambridge, Mass.
May 1978   H.L.

Contents

General
X-Efficiency Theory
and Economic Development

1 | Neoclassical Theory and Development Economics

When a new problem arises it is natural for economists to use the theory they know in their attempts to analyze it. This was true in the Great Depression of the 1930s until Keynes's *General Theory* came along. When economic development became a significant topic after World War II, it was almost second nature for economists to try to apply conventional microtheory or macrotheory to the new set of problems. After all, we can hardly expect economists to apply theories that do not exist. But this general approach presents difficulties, as well as ambivalent behavior on the part of members of the profession. For example: those who were somewhat less encumbered by theoretical blinders saw or believed they observed surplus labor in agriculture in developing countries while those more under the influence of the pattern of beliefs that underlie conventional microtheory believed that surplus labor and a positive wage rate was a logical impossibility and hence an empirical mirage. Whatever the truth may be in this particular case, the conflict that arose illustrates part of the problem. The nature of the argument frequently appeared to be whether the empirical assertions were correct or not. But a basic question, raised rather infrequently, was to ask whether the theory was really relevant to the problem at hand.

In my own work it seemed to me that the question of the appropriateness of the theory was frequently the critical question. To what extent was conventional microtheory really applicable to the analysis of the types of problems frequently faced by developing countries? The purpose of this book is to show that at least for some types of problems faced by developing countries, a broader and more general theory than the conventional one is likely to be more relevant to a number of issues at hand.

Conventional microtheory is a highly refined product of over a century of evolution. The most sharply honed variant, as well as the most representative version, is the model of the perfectly competitive industry.

The mind set of most economists in approaching new problems is determined to a great extent by the mode of analysis derived from the competitive model. Even in cases where it is not clear initially which model may apply, the mode of thinking that underlies the competitive model is likely to be used, at least in part, simply because of the absence of alternatives. It is, therefore, important and useful to examine some of the significant postulates behind the competitive model to see how they relate to normal problems of development.

It is impossible to state all of the assumptions behind the traditional model, however, some of the following observations are of interest. The model assumes that the basic actors or "economic agents" are households or firms and that these agents make rational decisions in the sense that they attempt to maximize the value of some variable subject to various constraints. Thus under all circumstances they try to do as well as they possibly can. All relevant information to make the decisions is assumed to be available. The normal outcome of the process is a set of inputs, outputs, and prices. Some of the most important phenomena explained by the model are the *allocation* of inputs to firms made on the basis of price signals, the choice of techniques to be used in production, and the quantities of goods purchased by households.

Now let us look briefly at some of the important aspects which are not considered in the conventional theory. How effectively the inputs are utilized in *producing* the goods does not enter as a variable. Here it is important to make a distinction that traditional theory does not make, that is, the distinction between the purchase of inputs by a firm and the degree of effectiveness of their use in the firm. The basic example is the purchase of labor *time* (for a certain payment per week) versus the actual *effort* that the individual worker actually puts forth. The same distinction can be made of other services. Obviously, equipment of various sorts could be used more or less effectively, used for more or less hours per day, maintained in better or worse condition, placed in more or less convenient locations in terms of effectiveness, and so on. The main line theory assumes that firms minimize costs and hence inputs will be used as effectively as possible. Thus, the question of the degree of the effectiveness of the utilization of inputs cannot even be raised as a question within the traditional theory. But is this question unimportant?

A second aspect to be considered is how quickly a new technique of production will be adopted after it becomes available. Will it be adopted as soon as it is economical to do so? If we find that this is not the case, in fact, then conventional theory has nothing to say on this question. Yet I would argue that in developing countries there are innumerable instances in which innovations are not adopted when it pays to do so, but the conventional model does not allow us to analyze this question.

A related question is how imperfections in the market affect the sort of economic activities that are carried out, and how these activities are compared to the ones that are not performed because of market imperfections. Once market imperfections are introduced, traditional theory has little to say. An exception is those cases for which all imperfections are attributable to monopolies and the monopoly analysis is allowed to take over. However, even for these cases, we should argue that a deficiency of monopoly analysis is that it assumes cost minimization.

We have indicated three types of questions which may be of significance to economic growth in developing countries but which cannot be readily handled on the basis of traditional microtheory. Basically, these three general questions do not involve the process of allocating resources to firms, and in some instances they cannot be handled on the basis of rational reactions to price signals. Given the difficulties we have considered it is not surprising that so much work in the study of economic development has been carried out on the basis of macro models rather than micro. Nevertheless, as the following chapters will indicate, the micro aspects of development cannot be ignored. The question of the appropriate theory for micro analysis remains a significant issue.

Having indicated some of the assumptions of traditional microtheory and some of the questions which are significant for development problems, we can now examine the extent to which these questions are answered by the conventional approach. First, we notice that the conventional microtheory in using the concept of an economic agent does not distinguish between the single-person firms and multi-person firms. All size firms fall under the rubric of economic agents. But do these different size firms really operate on the basis of the same principles? Consider the case of medium to large size multi-person firms. Can we assume that in such firms as "economic agents" really minimize costs? It seems reasonable not to make this assumption so that at the very least we can raise the questions about the degree of effectiveness with which inputs are used.

A number of elements are involved in the question of cost minimization. On the one hand, the mere size of the firm may make it impossible for any decision maker to take into account all the elements necessary to make cost minimization decisions and to carry them out. If it is impossible to do so and some other decision procedure is used, we should examine to what extent this procedure deviates from the cost minimization and how it influences the degree of effectiveness of input use. Equally important, the decision may not be made by an individual. It may be made formally by committees, or informally by groups of various sorts. Once again, cost minimization may make sense for individual decision making but not for group decision making. Finally, an individual's personality may be such that he or she does not wish to undergo the effort involved in maximization or minimization decision making and behavior. Hence, there may be situational and personality reasons for not assuming that cost minimization takes place. We could think of a variety of circumstances under which we may want to question cost minimization and hence want to examine individual personalities and organizational procedures which determine the degree of effectiveness of input use. What should be clear is that different degrees of utilization can give different results in terms of output. Thus, for two similar economies *A* and *B,* it may be possible that incentives are such that, although inputs are allocated similarly in both cases, they are utilized differently so that the level of output is much higher in *A* than in *B*. This is a significant question for developing economies.

The study of economic development directly focuses attention on the problems of changes of level of output rather than explaining the actual output *level*. Hence, an especially important question is to what extent do economies respond to opportunities which result in *changes* in the level of output? Two elements are especially significant: (1) the rate of innovation and (2) the rate of investment.

The rate of innovation is normally viewed as depending upon the profitability of the various innovate options. But is

that all it depends upon? Will profitable innovations always
be adopted? At the very least, this is a question that should be
asked. Hence, the need for a framework of analysis that allows
us to ask this particular question. Conventional microtheory
does not permit us to ask this question, since it assumes that
profitable innovations will always be adopted. This is an obvious corollary to the usual profit maximizing postulate. We
will also show that the concept of entrepreneurship which is in
part related to the adoption of innovations becomes exceptionally fragile in conventional microtheory.

We shall try to show in a later chapter that a generalized
version of X-efficiency theory allows us to take into account the
adoption of innovations without assuming that they are adopted
as soon as they are profitable. The main difficulty with the conventional microtheory is that it assumes away many aspects of
reality which are especially significant in determining the rate
of growth of developing countries. Nobody really expects that
people will always respond affirmatively and immediately to
profitable options. At the very least we expect some degree of
inertia to be operative. Whether the amount of inertia in any
system is so little as to be trivial or is so large as to be significant,
the degree of inertia is an important and empirical question.
In our view it is very frequently significant. There is quite a bit
of fragmented empirical evidence to support this view. There
are also numerable instances of personal observations. In any
event it seems worthwhile to try to develop a model under
which inertial influences and their possible significance can be
studied.

An important point to be kept in mind is that a small magnitude of inertia which influences growth may accumulate into
large amounts over a number of years. Consider briefly the case
of innovation. Suppose that in any one year only two percent
of the firms introduce an innovation. Suppose further that inertial elements reduce that to one and a half percent. In terms of
overall performance of the economy for a given year, this ap-

pears to be of a trivial magnitude. Only one economic unit in two hundred is involved. Nevertheless, it may influence twenty-five percent of the growth rate. Suppose that without inertial elements the growth rate would be four percent and with inertial elements the growth rate would drop by one percent. Assume further that in this economy there is a two percent rate of population growth. In other words, it cuts the per capita growth rate in half. What appears to influence only minute portions of the firms involved can be exceptionally significant in determining the long run growth of the economy. Other possibilities can be easily worked out under which a relatively small influence on the economy in any one year may have extremely important effects on the growth rate and on the level of economic well being one or two generations hence.

One of the curious aspects of the relationship of neoclassical theory to economic development is that in the conventional theory, entrepreneurs as they are usually perceived play almost no role. Let us recall that according to the neoclassical theory all of the options are known and the prices of inputs and outputs are also known. It follows that all a potential entrepreneur really has to do is merely to calculate possible outcomes and make his decisions. Entrepreneurship seems to be reduced to a trivial activity. Yet, at the same time, in the real world there is a general belief, and a correct one, that entrepreneurial skills are quite rare and that activities carried out by entrepreneurs are important in determining how well economies operate. In the real world in which we live, we operate on the basis of significant market imperfections. While the last factor is certainly true for developed economies, it is all the more important for developing countries. After all, one important aspect of the process of development is the improvement in markets and the reduction of market imperfections. A theory that does not allow for significant imperfections prevents us from analyzing the importance of the entrepreneurial role. It is beliefs of this sort that are behind our attempt in a later chapter to develop a theory of entrepreneurship in which market imperfections play a significant role, and in which entrepreneurs overcome various imperfections in the market.

A summary way of stating some of the issues raised in this chapter, and developed in detail in the rest of this book, is to say that we plan to look *into* the "black box" of microtheory to see if it is adequate for the analysis of economic development problems. The black box is a decision making entity which follows maximization or optimization rules. Once the correct decision is made it is presumed that to whatever degree performance is required, that performance of the type that the decision requires in fact takes place. The basic notion behind the black box is that we do not look into it. We presume it does its decision-making job according to the externally presumed rules irrespective of the nature of its internal system. The black box notion is, in fact, a felicitous metaphor for a critical aspect of neoclassical theory. It represents the complete mechanization of the decision-making process, but the mechanism avoids some difficult questions. And because it is purely mechanical it appears rather inhuman.

If we are to judge the black box metaphor, we have to inquire how close the black box is to real behavior. The answer is likely to depend on two aspects: (1) the problem under consideration and (2) the real nature of the decision making entity. With respect to the latter the black box comes closest to reality in situations in which the household or firm (or decision making entity) is a single individual who has a great deal of information about the alternative options and is motivated to choose rationally and in which the choice itself is tantamount to, or synonymous with, performance. In cases of trade between individuals where the price is set by some sort of an auctioning procedure and individuals choose only the quantities they wish to buy and sell, we have a situation in which the black box metaphor may be very close to reality. For the most part the nature of the example assumes away the question of performance. In the case in which goods have to be produced performance no longer necessarily follows choice automatically. Indeed, the contrived nature of the example reveals not only the limitations of the black box metaphor but also why it is desirable to reconsider how the black box is likely to operate in somewhat more complex situations.

The question of performance and its relation to decision making is worth investigating in some detail. Consider the case in which goods are produced in a factory of an individual owner-manager. The owner-manager has to make at least three types of decisions: (1) the choice of the prices and quantities of the inputs to be purchased, (2) the choice of the prices and quantities of the outputs that he sells, and (3) the transformation of inputs into outputs. In transforming inputs into outputs the owner-manager presumably has to choose a "technique of production." The first and second decisions above represent choices, but the third decision is more complex. It is true that we may visualize the transformation of inputs into outputs as involving the choice of a technique of production, but something much more important is involved. There is not only the initial decisions involved, but also an extremely significant area of performance. It does not do much good to argue, as economists sometimes do in elementary textbooks, that actual performance is a matter of engineering and that as economists we are only interested in the choice aspect. This approach simply allows us to avoid understanding a significant aspect of economic behavior. The process we call performance not only involves *doing* things, but it allows for new choices to be made every step of the way.

Consider the construction of a building. This too can be fitted into the rubric of choice of inputs, choice of outputs, and choice of production techniques. The contractors may have received plans from the architect about the nature of the building and may have agreed on the price at which the building is to be constructed and delivered to the owners. Suppose that the agreed upon construction period is six months. Is that the end of the economist's interest in the matter? Hardly, if the economist really wants to understand all the aspects of the process so as to understand the economics of the construction industry. At every step of the way during the six month construction period (if it takes no more than six months), *new* economic decisions are made. It is one thing to determine the inputs that are to be purchased, it is something else to use them effectively in the construction of the building. Furthermore, it is one thing to presume to have chosen a technique of production, it is something else to carry it out according to that technique. Over the six month period the contractor and his employees will face a host of incentives to cut corners and to use materials and techniques in such a way so that the building turns out to be of somewhat lower quality than originally anticipated by the owners. How it all works out is not our concern at this point. Enough has been said to indicate that the process we call performance itself yields a host of opportunities for new economic decisions. The initial decisions and performance in the light of these new decisions are not at all the same thing.

We have already suggested that in some sense firms make initial price, quantity, and (in some cases) technique decisions in multi-person firms. But the details of the quantity and technique decisions have to be worked out by a number of individuals who put forth effort. Detailed effort decisions are made all along the way, and it is these detailed effort decisions which determine the performance and growth of the economy in the long run. We must also determine to what extent technique decisions may be said to be made initially.

A distinction ignored by the black box metaphor is the one between principals and agents. It should seem almost self-evident that in making detailed effort decisions the motivations are quite different whether the individual involved is making the decision for himself as a principal or if he is making it for someone else, as it were, as an agent. There is no reason to assume that principals and agents have identical interests or that agents adopt the interests of their principals. In fact there is frequently good reason to presume that different interests are involved. Hence we should expect different effort levels on the part of the agent compared to those of the principal even if the other circumstances in the context are the same. In examining development problems it would seem especially important in many contexts to distinguish between principals and agents and to see the extent to which performance differs given (1) the nature of the agent-principal relationship and (2) the distribution and responsibilities of agents within the organized production units involved.

Of course, the conventional theory, including the black-box metaphor, normally ignores the question of effort altogether. It is not completely clear what the appropriate underlying assumption should be with respect to effort. One reasonable interpretation, in keeping with the other assumptions of microtheory, is that all labor contracts, whether formal or informal, involve *given* and *agreed upon* effort levels and that individuals always perform in accordance with these agreed upon levels. However, in the real world all labor contracts are incomplete. Effort levels are rarely if ever specified in every respect. Even limited observation suggests that in some regards, the effort of those hired on a time basis is a discretionary variable. It would, therefore, seem reasonable that an appropriate analytical structure should treat effort as a discretionary variable within limits. This is precisely the fundamental postulate of the X-efficiency theory which is described in the next chapter. We shall see that it is useful to examine a number of economic development problems from the viewpoint of this postulate.

RELATIONS BETWEEN VARIOUS CHAPTERS

The next chapter sets out the nature of general X-efficiency theory. This will be the basic approach to be applied to the various development problems considered in chapters three to eight. These last six chapters can be viewed in two ways: (1) as applications of X-efficiency theory and (2) as the presentation of interrelated economic problems. They represent applications of general X-efficiency theory to a variety of development problems. As a development economist, I have been interested in most of the problems for a long period of time, and I viewed them initially from a conventional theoretical viewpoint. It seems to me that the application of X-efficiency theory makes these problems more tractable intellectually than they had been heretofore. This in itself may be a sufficient raison d'être for both the choice of the problems and the nature of the book. However, the problems are not randomly chosen. There is some rough rhyme and reason to their selection and to their interconnections.

To see the relations between them it is important to keep in mind that economic theory (and economic development analysis) does not have a natural sequence. Its nature is not like the telling of a story. Instead, it is a system of simultaneous causation. In economics the system of analysis is much closer to that of a jigsaw puzzle. There are a great many pieces that fit together, but there is no unique or special sequential way in which one piece has to fit another. One can start at a great many places. When enough pieces have been fitted together the general nature of the picture unfolds. In the same sense it is probable that various sequences of these chapters might have worked equally well. Some readers might have preferred some sequences to others. What matters is not the sequence but the possible interconnections which we will now discuss.

In general, the six chapters are concerned with the ways in which human inputs affect economic development. We visualize development as a process, various aspects of which occur simultaneously. Central to this process is the way in which, and the extent to which, people are marshalled into various enterprises which produce the products that determine the rate of development. From this viewpoint it seems reasonable to consider first the nature of entrepreneurship in the development process (chapter three). While at the outset we consider entrepreneurship in isolation of the other chapters, the supply of entrepreneurship is a factor that we should keep in mind in the chapters that follow. The next four chapters involve closely related processes.

The existence of surplus labor creates pressure on agricultural manpower, which results in a flow of migrants from the agricultural sector to urban areas. In addition, this flow to the urban areas simultaneously helps to create part of the problem of urban unemployment, as well as the problem of employment absorption. In part, the employment absorption problem may be viewed as a failure of entrepreneurship, but it can also be viewed as a failure either to induce enough savings, to absorb enough investment, or to choose sufficient labor-using techniques so that full employment could be achieved. Hence, the connections are made between chapter six on the relations between investment absorption, innovation, and choice of technique, and the related problem of employment absorption, surplus agricultural labor (chapter four) and migration (chapter five).

Behind the employment and migration problems lies the pressure created by population growth and its corollary, labor force growth (chapter seven). The central variable considered in this area is the fertility rate. It therefore seems reasonable to include the theory of fertility as the central part of the processes of population growth and population pressure.

Finally, in the last chapter, we turn to a theme underlying both entrepreneurship, employment and investment absorption —the nature of the organization of enterprise and, especially, state-run enterprises. In other words, the various processes that determine development have to be seen in terms of not only the fact that there are firms which produce goods, employ workers, determine investment, and so on, but that the entire process depends to a considerable degree on the incentives generated within an organization, and by the environment in which the organization exists.

One final thought must be kept in the minds of the readers.

All of this represents research on the frontier, as it were. Such research, by its very nature, has to be somewhat tentative. It naturally results in a somewhat lesser degree of tidy integration of all of its elements than the type of economic writing which involves the restatement and clarification of themes considered for decades or centuries.

2 | General X-Efficiency Theory

We shall refer to the reformulation of microtheory, presented here in skeletal outline, as general X-efficiency theory. One reason for this name is that the theory helps to explain the phenomenon of X-efficiency, but this understates the generality and nature of the theory to be presented. The degree of generality of X-efficiency theory is suggested in the pages that follow when we compare neoclassical microtheory and X-efficiency theory and indicate how the former may be viewed as a special case of the latter.

The X-efficiency idea, in a narrow sense, is an extremely simple one. Suppose that certain inputs have been allocated to a firm. These inputs can be used with various degrees of effectiveness within the firm. The more effectively they are used the greater the output. When an input is not used effectively, the difference between the actual output and the maximum output attributable to that input is a measure of the degree of X-inefficiency. In this context X-efficiency is to be contrasted with allocative efficiency, the latter being the form of efficiency commonly considered in neoclassical economics. The basic notion is that we must distinguish between the allocation of inputs to legal decision making units (such as firms and households) and the effective use of these inputs within such decision making units. Of course, effective use depends simultaneously on both the decisions that are made on *how* to use inputs and the actual performance based on these decisions. Thus, within the firm, the concept of X-inefficiency captures both the detailed decision making process which may determine the intent of how to use inputs and the actual performance aspect.

Another way of looking at X-inefficiency is in terms of the inputs needed to produce a predetermined output by a firm. This is illustrated in figure 2.1. The value of the minimum inputs needed is designated as V_o. The actual inputs needed is designated by V_a. The ratio of the difference between the two over the actual expenditure, $(V_a - V_o)/V_a$ is also a measure of X-inefficiency.

For purposes of this book we want a somewhat broader notion of X-inefficiency than the one that looks at the problem in terms of given allocated inputs and their utilization. Part of the inputs available to a firm is knowledge of opportunities open to it, or the information on how to obtain such knowledge. Thus, the deviation between the value of maximizing the opportunities open to the firm and those actually utilized is also part of the X-inefficiency phenomenon.

GENERAL STRUCTURE OF THE THEORY

To show at a glance as it were how our theory differs from the conventional theory the following table may be helpful. In table 2.1 we list various components of X-efficiency theory and next to each component the status of the related components in neoclassical theory. Table 2.1 is not intended to be complete. In preparing the table a special effort was made to keep down the number of components so that one could keep in mind a limited set of elements as various aspects of the theory are considered.

Since the table is not likely to be self-explanatory, a few remarks may be in order to indicate the nature of some of these components and their relation to each other. At the outset we note that under X-efficiency theory the basic unit is the individual rather than the firm or the household. In addition, the individual is not assumed to maximize income or anything else. The performance will depend on the personality which is characterized in the next section under the rubric of selective rationality. For present purposes we simply assume that individual

Figure 2.1

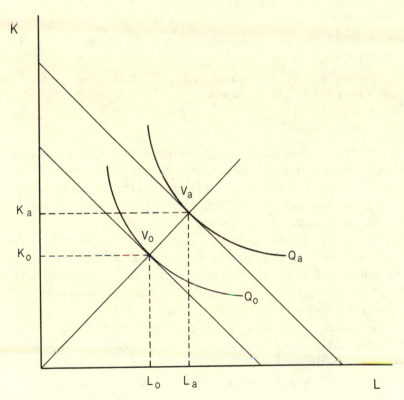

$$V_o = K_o L_o$$
$$V_a = K_a L_a$$

Table 2.1

Components	X-Efficiency Theory	Neoclassical Theory
1. Units	1. Individuals	1. Households and firms
2. Psychology	2. Selective rationality	2. Maximization or minimization
3. Effort	3. Discretionary variable	3. Assumed given
4 Inert areas	4. Important variable	4. None
5. Interpersonal interactions	5. Some	5. None
6. Agent-principal relationship	6. Differential interests	6. Identity of interests
7. Cost impactor/ impactee relations	7. Impactors not equal to impactees	7. Not relevant or impactors identical to impactees

personalities choose (in a sense) the degree to which they are interested in pursuing purposive behavior. We observe also that *effort,* which is presumed to be predetermined in neoclassical theory, becomes a significant discretionary variable under X-efficiency theory.

The concept of inertia plays a critical role in general X-efficiency theory. It is developed formally in that theory through the concept of inert areas. Clearly, a perusal of standard textbooks on neoclassical theory shows that there is no counterpart inertial concept in the neoclassical model.

The usual assumption in neoclassical theory is that every decision making unit is independent of all other decision making units. While such units interact within the market with the price system, they do not interact directly through pressure, emulation, personal competition, or similar influences. In X-efficiency theory, where individuals are the basic units, we assume that such interactions do play a role.

The distinction between principals and agents is either not made in conventional theory or is an irrelevant distinction since the effort level is presumed given in all contracts. Once the effort level is a discretionary variable then this distinction becomes significant since the motivations of principals are likely to be quite different than the motivations of agents, and, as a consequence, their effort levels, in the same contexts, will also differ.

This brief discussion of some of the main differences behind the basic assumptions of X-inefficiency theory as against the neoclassical model is intended only to indicate the basic structural differences between the two types of theories so that they may be kept in mind as we fill in the details of the general X-efficiency theory.

SELECTIVE RATIONALITY

The term, selective rationality, suggests that (1) there are degrees of rationality and (2) that in some sense individuals have a choice as to how "rational" they are to behave in different contexts. The extent to which they will be rational, *on the average,* depends on personality. Thus we have in mind that there are different degrees of rationality between which individuals may choose to govern their behavior in specific contexts. Consider the case where someone is pursuing a specific objective which allows for variations in some dimension. The extent to which the person will persevere along that dimension will depend on the personality. If one perseveres as much as possible, this may be viewed as "fully rational" behavior. Only in such a case is the individual acting as a maximizer. We recognize circumstances under which people choose to persevere less fully than the extent possible, but it is important to note that a deviation from fully rational behavior does not connote irrationality. Selectively rational behavior is not inferior to that which is fully rational.

A specific area within which there are frequent deviations

between maximizing behavior and actual behavior is behavior that determines personal health maintenance. It is frequently presumed that individuals wish to be as healthy as possible. However, actual behavior in many cases seems to go counter to this postulate. Consider the following three areas of behavior that influence health: (1) weight maintenance, (2) smoking, and (3) physical exercise. A great many individuals are aware that they are overweight, that they shouldn't smoke, and/or that they exercise infrequently or inadequately. Furthermore, they are aware of the behavioral changes that are required to maximize health maintenance. To a great many people health is exceedingly important, and the behavior modifications required to maintain health involve relatively small economic costs compared to people's interest in health maintenance. This is a clear cut case under which the maximization of health maintenance frequently does not take place. Obviously people's personalities and the contexts in which they live allow them to choose different degrees of health maintenance. Just as people choose less than maximum health maintenance, so in a similar manner we will argue that in many contexts people choose different degrees of less than full rationality.

Our basic postulate is that individuals make compromises between behaving the way they would like to, without constraints, and behaving the way they feel they *ought* to. The idea of going on a consumption spree represents behaving as one would like to. Watching one's budget and living fully within the constraints one believes the budget imposes constitute behavior in terms of the way one feels one ought to. Actual behavior usually involves a compromise between these two extremes.

A basic element of rational behavior is *constraint concern*. Economic behavior usually involves opportunities for gain, in some sense, but is subject to constraints of various sorts. Thus, consumers give up money income for goods which they enjoy more than cash, but they are still subject to the constraints of their budgets. Similarly, economic theory assumes that managers may try to maximize the profits of the firm subject to costs of allocating and using inputs effectively. It is important to note that concern about constraints is frequently unpleasant and that there is a tendency, especially for some types of personalities, to avoid complete constraint concern.

We shall use the concept *constraint concern* to include the opportunities as well as the constraints attached to these opportunities. Thus rational behavior involves persevering with respect to opportunities that yield the greatest payoff in some sense and at the same time being concerned with constraints to whatever degree necessary to obtain the greatest payoff. When we shall speak of less than complete rationality, we will have in mind less than complete perseverance in the pursuit of the opportunities and less than complete concern for the constraints involved in this context. This bundle of ideas is so interwoven that we have to consider all the ideas simultaneously to use the concept of constraint concern.

A concept that is related to constraint concern is the feeling of pressure. This may arise out of the dictates of an individual's conscience or through interpersonal relations. The less the level of constraint concern shown by an individual, the more pressure one is likely to feel. For example, if we view paying one's bills as an aspect of constraint concern, then related to that may be the feeling of pressure—the fewer bills paid the higher the pressure level and vice versa. Thus we can visualize a trade-off between the degree of constraint concern and pressure. Similarly, when we consider interpersonal relations we can visualize a trade-off between peer demands on individuals and the pressure a person might feel in accordance with the degree to which he or she acquiesces to such interpersonal demands.

These basic ideas are formalized in figure 2.2. The set of curves in the right quadrant marked $I_1, I_2 . . I_n$ represent the id curves which generalizes "spree" like behavior. These curves are basically indifference curves between felt pressure and constraint concern. They are drawn in such a way as to reflect the

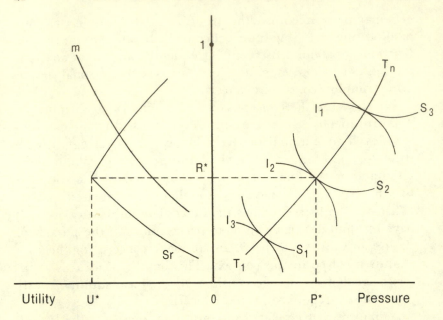

Figure 2.2

idea that increases in pressure would be traded for less constraint concern. The utility of these indifference curves increase towards the origin in the sense that people generally prefer less constraints and less pressure simultaneously. The id indifference curves marked $I_1 \ldots I_n$, $U(I_1)$, $U(I_2)$, $\ldots U(I_n)$ reflect higher utility values as we move *towards* the origin. This is consistent with the idea that people are likely to prefer both less constraint concern and less pressure.

We also assume that individuals are subject to internalized controls which reflect their standards of behavior. These standards impose on an individual obligations to his role, obligations to others, and so on. They reflect one's conscience or superego. We refer to the set of curves that reflect these ideas as an individual's superego curve. In figure 2.2 the set of equi-utility curves are marked $S_1 \ldots S_n$, $U(S_1)$, $U(S_2)$, $U(S_3)$, $\ldots U(S_n)$. These curves have higher utility values as we move away from the origin. This reflects the idea that in terms of their *ideals,* individuals wish to be more purposive, more constraint concerned, and so on. The slope on any point on any one of the S curves reflects a willingness to trade a little more pressure for a little less constraint concern. The tangencies of the id and superego curves reflect superior positions to some nontangent points; i.e., for every point off the tangency locus there exists a point on the locus that is superior.

The locus of such tangencies, $T_1, T_n,$ reflects a set of internal moral compromises between which an individual would choose to control his behavior. Each point reflects some degree of compromise between an individual's vision of himself as a person who meets his internal standards and his desire to do as he *pleases*—that is, a desire to pursue pleasures at the expense of constraints and obligations. In the left quadrant of figure 2.2 we show the net utility values of the points on $T_1 T_n,$ that is, each point represents the difference between $U(S)$ for that point and $U(I)$ for that point.

Some remarks are in order on the interpretation of figure 2.2. First and foremost we must keep in mind that this figure represents a characterization of personality. In other words, it indicates how a particular personality *feels,* on the average, about handling constraint concerns that surround opportunities. In the left quadrant of figure 2.2, we show one curve labelled m and one curve labelled sr. If we look at the curve m, we note that this reaches its highest utility at the point of "full" rationality, (i.e., constraint concern $= 1$). Hence, such a personality will be a maximizing individual. On the other hand, a personality that reflects the curve labelled sr reaches highest utility at a level of constraint concern labelled R^*, which represents less than maximizing behavior and less than full rationality. Thus, the personality reflected by the sr curve implies nonmaximizing behavior.

We should note that statements about personality are not the same as statements about choice *within* an economic context. There is no definite connection between *utility* used in characterizing personality and *utilities* which may be involved in determining choice. It is the fundamental responsibility of the personality statements to govern choice behavior but they are not part of the values of the alternatives between which choices are made. Hence if a certain personality selects to behave, on the average, by deviations from the fully rational level, then in making choices the individual will not behave in a maximizing fashion. A corollary of this type of behavior involves a willingness to incur costs where strict maximizing behavior will dictate the avoidance of such costs. For example, charitable behavior would not be rational on strictly maximizing assumptions.

The following implications about the nature of selective rationality should be kept in mind as we proceed to outline other aspects of X-efficiency theory.

1. The concept of constraint concern includes components which involve a sense of obligation an individual has to his own self-interest, as against the obligations he has to the interests of the firm, which do not always coincide with the former. The less the degree of constraint concern, the less, on the average, an individual will feel a sense of obligation to what he views to be the interests of the firm.

2. The greater the degree to which an individual's actual constraint concern level is beyond U^*, the greater the resistance he will offer having his degree of constraint concern increased further.

3. If external performance standards fall, this will shift the S curves in figure 2.2 towards the origin, and the curve U^* will move accordingly towards the origin. This process will be employed in later sections when we discuss the concept of effort entropy.

PRINCIPAL-AGENT RELATIONS AND EFFORT CHOICE

In conventional microtheory all economic activity takes place between principals, or, to the extent that agents exist, they are presumed to act entirely in accord with the interests of the principals. In fact in most textbook treatments no distinction is made between principals and agents and the entire discussion is in terms of economic decision units which behave in their own interests. Once we shift away from the firm as the basic decision unit and consider the individual as the basic entity, the distinction between principals and agents becomes important. Agents may make decisions in the interests of their principals, but they may also make decisions which emphasize their own interests irrespective of whether they are in the principals' interest. There is no reason to presume that the contractual relationship between agents and principals is either a complete one or is one that necessarily prevents the agents from deviating from maximizing the principals' interests. In any type of complex society with multi-person firms, agents are likely to have opportunities to pursue their own interests in such a way that they deviate to some degree from maximizing the interests of their principals.

Consider further, the individual in the context of being a member of a multi-person firm. What is expected of an individual under such circumstances? To be put very briefly the individual has to interpret his job in the firm so that it meets to some degree the expectations of others in the firm who have significant relationships with the individual. The usual example is the supervisor-supervisee relationship. The individual gets a job in the firm, as it were; there is someone he recognizes as his "boss"; there are frequently other individuals he recognizes as his peers; the firm membership or employment contract is usually incomplete and vague. From both his supervisor and his peers, he is likely to receive incomplete information as to what is expected of him; somehow he has to interpret this incomplete information so as to meet simultaneously his own desires and to some degree the desires of supervisors and peers. This is true of every individual in the firm in the sense that everyone associated with the firm has to interpret his or her job. One way of interpreting this formally is to say that everyone has to pick an *effort position*.

Before we explain the concept of an effort position, we must examine the concept of effort itself from an economic view-point. Clearly people not only make decisions as part of their economic activity but they also do various things. In other words they put forth effort in pursuit of economic objectives. In fact, we should view decision making itself as an effortful activity. This view fits psychological theory much better than the view of decision making as effortless and costless phenomena.[1]

It may be useful to classify the components of effort into the following four categories:

A, the actual activities that define the nature of the effort.

P, the pace per unit of time at which each activity is carried out.

Q, the quality with which activity is carried out.

T, the temporal sequence and time duration of carrying out the activity.

For the most part we will assume that time duration is given and hence temporal sequence is all that is involved here. Thus at any specific time we may define the carrying out of a job in terms of an $APQT$ bundle or what we shall refer to as an effort point. In other words, each effort point involves a specific activity-pace-quality-time bundle.

For any individual there exists an infinity of effort points to choose from. By a "job interpretation" we visualize the choice of a subset of effort points which we will refer to as an effort position. In principle the effort position may contain only one effort point. But we would expect the average job interpretation

---

[1] In conventional theory the relationship between decisions and "doings" is not spelled out. Economics is about decisions and decisions are normally viewed as costless and effortless. One way of spelling things out is to presume that the "doings" are always in accordance with prior decisions. But for many analytical purposes it may be useful not to have this complete dichotomy between decisions and "doings." For example, if effort is a variable, then in various stages in carrying out effort there may be opportunities for additional decisions about the extent to which further effort should take place. Hence some, perhaps most, decisions should be viewed as involving effort and as part of a larger effort choice made at an earlier stage.

to contain a number of effort points. The reason for this is that the individual would shift from one effort point to another depending on some signals received about the external demands for the individual's effort. This is not to presume that individuals are necessarily completely flexible or completely responsive to the demands of others, but the concept of a new effort position allows for some degree of responsiveness. Thus, to whatever degree an individual wishes to be responsive can be reflected in his choice of an effort position. We shall see later when we introduce the concept of inert areas that we assume that in the general case effort positions are stable to some degree.

The main reason for emphasizing the contrast between effort positions and effort points is the nature of the signals received by an employee (e.g., a verbal request, a written request, an order, a complaint, etc.) indicating varying *demands* for effort. When heeded, such signals, as usually interpreted, trigger what the individual believes to be the appropriate effort response or one that he likes to give. Aspects of the work context which could not be anticipated may be viewed by some individuals as signals to change effort, including the reduction of effort. However, we should *not* assume that individuals associate equal utility to all points in their effort positions.

For a variety of analytical purposes, it is useful to associate effort points to productivity values contributed by the effort and a utility value to the individual putting forth the effort including the utility of income from firm membership. It is to be emphasized that the productivity value may exist in some ex post sense, but that its existence is not necessarily known to either the individual putting forth the effort or to the firm for whom the individual presumably puts forth the effort. It is simply that for analytical convenience, it is sometimes useful to presume that the association between effort and productivity exists and that it can be determined.

In a similar spirit to the above, one can associate an *average* productivity value with an effort position and an *average* utility value with the same effort position. Since the effort positions may contain many effort points, we cannot necessarily associate unique productivity values and utility values with effort positions. For many analytical purposes the association of the average values is likely to be sufficient.

It is of interest to try to relate our psychological postulates to the choice of effort positions. Part of the traits which are the elements of constraint concern, as well as the central idea of constraint concern, suggest that in the choice of an effort position there will be a division of interest between the self-interest of the individual as against his devotion to the interest of the firm. We argued that the lower the degree of constraint concern, the greater the extent to which the effort position will reflect self-interest, and the less it will reflect devotion to the firm's interests. Thus, low constraint concern may be associated with a desire to supply relatively low levels of effort from the firm's viewpoint. This does not necessarily imply that the total level of effort will be low. The job may provide enough avenues of pursuing self-interest so that the choice of activities may produce a high level of effort, but not in terms of furthering the aims of the firm.

In figure 2.3 we illustrate the effort-utility relation for an individual. Three general ideas are involved in the way the curve Eu is drawn. We assume that up to a point utility increases as effort increases. In other words, the individual does not wish to be doing absolutely nothing in preference to doing something. Beyond some point, as effort increases still further, utility declines, which assumes that at the margin more effort is somewhat irksome as compared to less effort. Finally, we have drawn the relation with a relatively "flat top." This is presumed to reflect nonextreme personalities. In other words, it reflects the idea that around the optimum effort level individuals are likely to be fairly flexible with respect to putting forth a little more or a little less effort. The normal demands of life are likely to be such that variations in effort are required in order to handle different situations. Well balanced individuals are likely to be responsive to such situations without extreme changes in their utility level. Similarly the shift from work to nonwork situations also requires changes in effort levels. If these transitions are to be carried out smoothly, they should involve relatively small changes in utility. This is not to argue that all

Figure 2.3

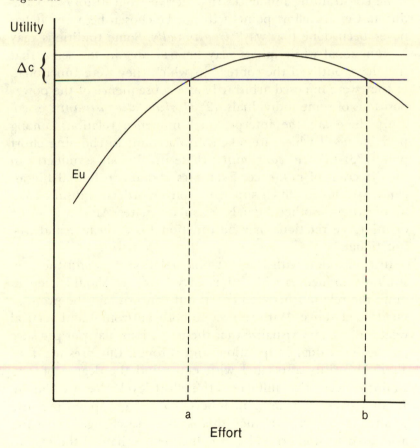

Δc = Utility cost of moving from a to b

personalities will have flat top effort utility relations but simply that for those who are selected for most types of jobs this will probably be the case. Thus, the flat top relation represents a norm around which other more extreme relationships between utility and effort are likely to exist.

We now turn to consider interpersonal influences on the effort-utility relation. We distinguish three categories of *constraining* influences. (1) *Traditional constraints:* these represent those constraining influences that derive from history and tradition. Certain effort points will not be chosen because "it has never been done that way" *traditionally*. Some traditions may be functional while others may be *arbitrary* in the sense that they have outlived the context in which they were functional, or they were imposed arbitrarily as a consequence of the power positions of some individuals. (2) *Horizontal constraints:* essentially these are the interpersonal influence relations among peers, some of which are taken into account in choosing effort points. (3) *Vertical constraints:* these involve an asymmetry in the direction of influence. Examples abound in formal hierarchical systems in which superiors convey orders, transmit communications or other "signals" to subordinates. All constraining or influence relations may be functional or *arbitrary* and dysfunctional.

In connection with interpersonal relationships and the constraining influences which they may have, we should keep in mind the relation between constraint concern and the pressure mentioned above. With respect to both horizontal and vertical relations, we may visualize that these relations may put pressure on the individual in question, and through this pressure they alter the utility associated with effort and the degree of constraint concern that influences the effort levels that are chosen. If, for a given effort level, members of a peer group put pressure to alter the effort level then this is likely to change the utility associated with effort and as a consequence changes the overall effort-utility relation.

The traditional influences maintain some degree of continuity between existing effort levels and past effort levels. They help to insure some degree of predictability with respect to the effort-productivity relation. The horizontal constraints are likely to impose themselves on the more energetic workers in the firm, to reduce their norms towards somewhat lower levels and to increase the levels for especially unenergetic individuals. In other words, because of peer group disapproval, there will be a tendency to reduce the utility level on either side of the mean.

Similarly, the vertical relations are likely to involve attempts to move people to somewhat higher levels of effort from that imposed by peer group influences. The mere process of selection is likely to be in the direction of movement away from peer group values.

The utility value of effort levels beyond the mean is likely to depend on complex relationships. On the one hand if there is no conflict between peers and supervisory authority then the effect of the vertical constraints is likely to increase the utility values of effort levels beyond the main effort levels. On the other hand, if there exist peer group-authority conflicts then we are likely to have two forces which counteract each other. It would be difficult to tell in any abstract way which would turn out to be more important. However, for effort levels well below the mean, both the peer group and the vertical relation are likely to result in reducing utility values more than they otherwise would be.

THE THEORY OF INERT AREAS AND EFFORT ENTROPY

A critical element in our theory is the concept of *inert areas*. The inert area idea is related to human inertia. It depends, among other things, on some of the following considerations: the magnitude of the insensitivity area, the utility costs of decision making, and habitual position preference—i.e., the gradual habituation of doing things in a certain way, etc. In some contexts, it may be especially useful to distinguish two separate components of the inert area theory: (1) the utility cost of moving *away* from the present position—i.e., "packing up" costs, so to speak and (2) the utility cost of getting set up and "settling into," the new position.

We can visualize a set of points where the *inertial cost,* i.e., utility cost of shifting from any one point within the set to any other *within* that set, is greater than the utility gained. Such a set of points is an *inert effort area.* By the means already described an individual will choose a subset of the effort points from what he believes to be a known and allowable choice set in order to determine his effort position.

The fact that there is an inertial cost, i.e., the utility cost of a shift from one position to another implies that there is an area within the utility cost bounds such that movements from one position to another within these bounds will not take place. Opportunities for change which do not lead to a gain in utility (or to the avoidance of a loss of utility) greater than the cost of the shift will not be entertained.

The simplest view of the theory of inert areas is to assume that there is a fixed inertial cost irrespective of the size of the move. Unless otherwise indicated this is the concept we will employ whenever we use the term inert area. Clearly a number of variations on this basic idea could be introduced. For example, to some degree the inert area may depend on the time within an effort position, up to some maximum. Thus, the size of the inert area would increase with the elapse of time until it reached its maximum size. Similarly one could assume that the inertial cost depends in part on the "distance" of the move; moving may depend on two elements—some initial cost irrespective of size plus some additional cost which would be a function of distance. Adding these elements may in some cases add to the realism of inert area idea. But for illustrative purposes there would seem to be little need to introduce additional complications.

A final concept we wish to introduce is that of effort entropy.

We have already suggested that an individual would choose a set of effort points which will form his effort position. The reason many points are involved in an effort position is to meet a variety of demands for effort. Even though an effort position may be in an inert area, the degree to which effort points are used may gradually change over time and some points may fall into disuse. The basic idea is that not all points in the position are equally valued by the individual. Both superego considerations plus the interpersonal relationships, especially the vertical ones which involve supervisory relations, may change and their influence weaken. As a result some of the effort points with a lower utility than the average will gradually fall into disuse. Some of these effort points will involve activities which directly or indirectly monitor the activities of others. Hence, through these interpersonal effort influences, the monitoring system becomes attenuated, which in turn gives rise to other individuals' effort points falling into disuse. We refer to this process of the gradual atrophy of interpersonal effort relationships as *effort entropy*. In other words, we visualize an initial degree of interpersonal effort to possess a certain order or coherence and a tendency for this order or coherence to gradually atrophy unless managers or entrepreneurs struggle against the persistence of effort entropy. The significance of effort entropy is that it is one of the factors which causes gradually rising costs of production unless controlled by management.

ON EFFORT EQUILIBRIA

Once we have introduced the concept of the inert area then it is straightforward to relate that concept to the effort equilibrium of the individual. If an individual's effort position is in his inert area then this represents an equilibrium effort position. Clearly, it represents a position that will not be shifted unless there is strong external influences.

The effort equilibrium of the firm is a much more complex

idea because individuals play a dual role as a consequence of interpersonal interactions. That is to say, individuals not only choose effort positions, but they also influence the effort-utility relations of others through their participation in the system of interpersonal interactions. Consider the simple case of a two-person firm. It is not sufficient for each individual to choose an effort position that will be in his inert area. The nature of the inert areas and the effort utility relations will be influenced for each individual by the other individual. Hence, one of the conditions of equilibrium is that each individual's influence on the inert area of the other is such as to leave the chosen effort position within the inert area. For the firm this condition has to be generalized for all firm members. In other words, everyone's influence on everyone else must be sufficiently small so as not to alter the inert area in such a way so that the effort positions chosen remain within the inert areas. To see what is involved in an equilibrium state, it may help if we reflect on the possibility under which some effort points of an individual change the inert area of some other individual so that the effort position chosen by the second individual is no longer in his inert area. This last would not be an equilibrium state.

In addition to the micro-equilibrium considered above, we may visualize a macro-equilibrium which is of a somewhat different character. We consider the existence of some formal macro indices of behavior and control within the firm. These may be certain components of the financial statements of the firm. As long as the indices fall within the inert areas of those who are the formal managers of the firm, no formal attempts will be made to change anybody's behavior. The interesting aspects of formal macro-equilibrium lie in the possibility that the macro-equilibrium may coexist with a simultaneous micro-disequilibrium so that for a period of time the formal administrators may not notice underlying tensions and changes which may be taking place and which may eventually destabilize the macro-equilibrium.

EFFORT DECISIONS AND X-EFFICIENCY

Having set out the main outlines of the theory, we can specify briefly some of the sources of X-inefficiency derived from our model of the firm. Since individuals are interested in the utility of their effort positions and not necessarily in their productive contributions, we can readily see that the choice of effort positions based on utility would not in general yield maximum productivity from given inputs. In addition, since the average firm will contain agents as well as principals, and since we have already argued that agents will not necessarily perform in their principals' interests, but that they have interests of their own, we can readily see that the use of agents could be a source of inefficiency. We have also indicated that the representative individual will not necessarily maximize productivity, or anything else for that matter, and hence this may be a source of X-inefficiency even if the individual is a principal rather than an agent. Finally, the theory of inert areas suggests the possibility of the persistence of inferior effort positions even in the face of known superior alternatives. All of these are possible sources of X-inefficiency, but the relative importance of any of the specific sources may differ considerably in specific cases.

In addition to the points mentioned above, some aspects of the interpersonal interactions mechanism within the firm may also be sources of X-inefficiency. Consider the internal communications mechanism. For the effective utilization of inputs it is necessary that communications that have an impact on performance take place without hindrances between individuals and segments of the firm. In many cases *chains* of communication (within established channels) are involved. However, the concept of inert areas allows for the possibility that a channel of communication (in which different individuals are conduits) may be blocked at various points because the message enters the inert area of a "conduit" without coming out to continue the communication process. The same fate could befall the input of communications from outside the firm as well. Hence, to the extent that the flow of information, its assessment, and the processing of information contribute to the production processes, we can see that inert areas within communication channels can readily reduce efficiency and be causes of X-inefficiency.

The ideas developed in the previous paragraph are not only significant for well established production procedures and for the flow of information associated with such procedures, but are especially likely to be important for information that suggests new opportunities for economic gain. Thus, events which suggest opportunities for gain and the information surrounding such events may be missed, distorted, or not conveyed to areas where effective decisions could be made. These three aspects are all possibilities of a complex potential communication system which may not operate as effectively as it could.

To return to some of our basic notions, the effort position of firm members who should observe new opportunities may not contain the effort points to actually observe all of the opportunity information brought up by the environment. Similar possibilities exist with respect to processing information about opportunities received at some point so that they become distorted as they are transmitted within the organization. Similarly, at some point the flow of information will simply stop, whereas for optimal use it should have continued to other areas in the organization. The main emphasis of these remarks is that the same ideas that helped to explain why inputs are not used as effectively as they might be can also explain why less than full utilization of economic opportunities takes place on the part of individuals, firms, and the economy at large.

3 | Entrepreneurship and Development

The traditional theory of competition gives the impression that there is no need for entrepreneurship. If all inputs are marketed and their prices are known, and if all outputs are marketed and their prices known, and if there is a definite production function that relates inputs to outputs in a determinate way, we can always predict the profit for any activity that transforms inputs and outputs. Positive net profits should serve as a signal for entry into the market. The problem of marshaling resources and turning them into outputs appears to be a trivial activity. From this point of view it is hard to see why there should ever be a deficiency of entrepreneurship. But there is frequently a lack of entrepreneurship because the standard competitive model hides the vital functions of the entrepreneur.

Entrepreneurship is, of necessity, a rather elusive element in microeconomic theory.[1] We have already suggested that one reason for this is that there is little need for entrepreneurship as the word is normally understood *within* the assumptions of

[1] Peter Kilby, "Hunting the Hettalump," *Entrepreneurship and Economic Development*, 1971, pp. 2–4. The entire article provides an excellent review of the literature on the subject of entrepreneurship.

microtheory. If a state of disequilibrium exists under which there is excess demand, the cost of inputs to produce a product should be below the price level and only some elementary computations should be required for a potential entrepreneur to determine if it is worthwhile to enter the industry. It is not even clear that the entrepreneur as such would have to have any computing capacities since he could have someone to do the clerical work involved. Thus, if all markets are working well, and if all the information on inputs, production techniques, and outputs are well known, entrepreneurship becomes an extremely routine and unimportant function. In the light of these considerations, we can readily understand Frank Knight's efforts to find an ubiquitous function for the entrepreneur within the conventional theoretical framework. His achievement in trying to ascribe to the entrepreneur the unique capacity to undertake uncertainty is still the best description of an entrepreneur's role. Unfortunately it is not a very good description. Quite a few individuals who enter contracts face uncertainty without being entrepreneurs. In some cases, employees may face more uncertainty than employers, but it would be using words strangely indeed if we visualize employees as entrepreneurs. To get adequate results in the study of entrepreneurship, we must change some of the basic assumptions of microtheory.

The aim in what follows is twofold: to suggest a theory of entrepreneurship in which entrepreneurship has a unique and critical role; and to use this theory to indicate why entrepreneurship is significant in the development process.

We may distinguish two broad types of entrepreneurial activity: at one pole there is routine entrepreneurship, which is really a type of management; and at the other end of the spectrum, we have Schumpeterian or "innovational" entrepreneurship.[2]

By routine entrepreneurship we mean the activities involved

---

[2] See J. A. Schumpeter, "The Fundamental Phenomenon of Economic Development," *Entrepreneurship and Economic Development,* 1971, p. 43.

in coordinating and carrying on a well-established, going concern in which the parts of the production function in use (and likely alternatives to current use) are well known for a firm which operates in well-established and clearly defined markets.

By innovational entrepreneurship we mean the activities necessary to create (or carry on)[3] an enterprise where not all the markets are well established or clearly defined and/or in which the relevant parts of the production function are not completely known. In both the routine and the innovative cases, the entrepreneur coordinates activities that involve different markets; he is an *intermarket* operator. But in the case of innovative entrepreneurship not all of the markets exist or operate perfectly and the entrepreneur, if he is to be successful, must fill in for the market deficiencies.

THE DEMAND FOR ENTREPRENEURSHIP— OPPORTUNITIES FOR ENTREPRENEURIAL DEVELOPMENT

One of the main obstacles to our understanding of the entrepreneurial role lies in the conventional theory of the production function. This theory seems so reasonable at first blush that we are likely not to notice the subtle assumptions it makes. The basic culprits of misunderstanding are the following assumptions: that the complete set of inputs are specified and known to all actual or potential firms in the industry and that there is a fixed relation between inputs and outputs. The first assumption is implicit. To my knowledge, it is never stated explicitly, but I have not made an exhaustive search of the literature to check this. The second assumption is explicit, but it is rarely challenged.

In its usual conception the production function is considered to be clearly defined, fully specified, and completely known. Where and to whom in the firm this knowledge is supposed to

---

[3] Of course carrying on an enterprise is not quite the same as creating one. We shall consider the significance of this distinction later.

be available is never stated. In fact, there are great gaps of knowledge about the production function. Points on the production function refer to well-defined inputs. To the extent that these points are not completely defined in actuality, the entrepreneur must in some way make up the deficiency. Suppose that to produce a certain commodity, a certain type of machine has to be employed. If no one in the country produces such a machine and if imports are barred, only entrepreneurs who have access to information on how to construct the machine can enter the industry. The potential entrepreneur has to make up for a market deficiency. But that is not his only major function.

We have already suggested that if entrepreneurship is to be analyzed from an interesting viewpoint, we must change market assumptions. We must first visualize markets which are imperfect in a great many respects. Two types of imperfections are (1) obstacles to the marshaling of inputs and (2) gaps and holes in various input or output markets.

Obstacles may exist in a variety of ways. Some inputs may be available but are currently used for other purposes. It requires an active imagination to realize that something used for one purpose has superior or equally good alternative uses. Furthermore, the input may be available, but not for sale at any specific and known prices. In many cases the value of the input may not be known except in connection with the set of inputs which produces a valuable product in the market. In the last case there is clearly no advantage in examining the market input by input, since the need for the input (or inputs) can be seen from an adequate perspective only if viewed in connection with the potential marketing of the hitherto unmarketed product. Other obstacles that may exist include certain goods that are for sale to some individuals but not to others (e.g., credit may be available to some and not to others). The conditions of sale may not be equal to all individuals. The availability of credit is especially noteworthy in this connection.

Many gaps and holes that exist in the markets have to do with information. Thus, some techniques of production may not be known adequately even though the information and the skills necessary are obtainable. One can readily see that if we start with very imperfect markets, characterized by difficulties in or obstacles to obtaining some inputs and by market gaps with respect to others, the work is cut out for the imaginative and skillful entrepreneur. In these circumstances the entrepreneur has a very different job to do than in the case of perfect or even near perfect markets.

THE DEMAND FOR ENTREPRENEURSHIP—
X-EFFICIENCY AND THE SUPPLY OF ENTREPRENEURIAL CAPACITY

Our general X-efficiency theory suggests the possibility of an industry equilibrium which contains market imperfections as well as market gaps. Because of the existence of inert areas not all opportunities for profitable economic activities are filled. Furthermore the industry may be in the position in which not all costs are minimized. At the same time and a part of the same picture, firms do not fight effort entropy completely. Also, the suggestions that not all opportunities are filled implies that not all possible innovations are adopted. Thus, even under equilibrium there are economic opportunities for the display of entrepreneurial talent whether or not these opportunities are carried out.

Of course at any specific time not all industries will be in the type of equilibrium we have discussed above. As in conventional theory disequilibrium situations supply additional avenues for activity by entrepreneurs. In general we can see that both the equilibrium and disequilibrium conditions allow for the existence of holes in the enterprise network. We have also suggested that it may pay for firms to actually create market imperfections. As in conventional theory the creation of monopolies or monopsonies involve advantages to the firm able to get into such circumstances. But the monopolies of some create obstacles for others who are denied access to various types of inputs. Thus, we see that normal business activities under our general X-efficiency assumptions are responsible for the gaps and obstacles that may exist and persist within a market network.

Important inputs not well marketed are, for example, types of management and market knowledge. Even managers of the more routine type may not be available in well organized markets in many developing countries. Where available, their capacities may be very difficult to assess. One of the more important capacities of management is the ability to obtain and use factors of production that are not well marketed. In some countries the ability to obtain finance may depend on family connections rather than on the willingness to pay a certain interest rate. A successful entrepreneur may, at times, have to have the capacity to operate well in the political arena connected with his economic activities.

There is a significant relation between the entrepreneur's capacity and the fact that firms operate under some degree of slack. The existence of slack and the fact that not all inputs are marketed means that the market signals for profit opportunities are blurred. Since there is no one-to-one correspondence between inputs and outputs, a knowledge of output price and input prices can no longer yield the necessary signals. On the other hand, an error in perception can be partially counterbalanced by increased effort in marshaling resources and in operating the plant.

It is noteworthy that the traditional theory does not explain the existence of firms as time-binding entities. The theory presented here suggests that since the production function is incomplete, firms become valuable storehouses of detailed experience and knowledge. In part, this means that successful firms are entities that house successful motivational systems; these systems can be retained only through a scheme of renewable contractual arrangements of different time durations. It is in this way that the firm captures some of the long-term benefits of previous gap-filling and input-completing conquests.

A way of looking at the essential elements is to visualize the economy as a net made-up of nodes and pathways. The nodes represent industries or households that receive inputs (or consumer goods) along the pathway and send outputs (final goods and inputs for the other commodities) to the other nodes. The perfect competition model would be represented by a net that is complete; one that has pathways that are well marked and well defined, one that has well-marked and well-defined nodes, and one in which each element (i.e., firm or household) of each node deals with every other node along the pathways on equal terms for the same commodity. In the realistic model that we have in mind, there are holes and tears in the net, obstructions (knots) along the pathways, and some nodes and pathways, where they exist, are poorly defined and poorly marked or entirely unmarked from the viewpoint of elements of other nodes. We may refer to this net as impeded, incomplete, and "dark" in contrast to the unimpeded and "well lit" net that represents the competitive model. Of course, a portion of the real economy net may very loosely approximate the "unimpeded" net of the perfect competition model. Entrepreneurs working in the well-defined, non-hole, non-obstruction part of the net carry out routine entrepreneurial-managerial activities, while those who operate on the impeded, incomplete, and dark parts carry out new entrepreneurial activities. Entrepreneurial activities will make some portions of the net less impeded through extending markets (i.e., creating new pathways) but may make others more impeded through the creation of monopolies or the creation of other obstacles (e.g., high entry costs) where they previously did not exist. Inventions and the creation of new knowledge will to some extent extend the net to vague and incomplete areas, but other inventions may substitute relatively well-defined pathways and nodes for those which were previously ill defined and obstruction laden.

The view of the economy as a very imperfect network in which there are holes, obstacles, unequal access to pathways, and inefficient nodes helps us to see the supply of economic opportunities that may exist in the economy. But this is not the same as the effective demand for entrepreneurship. In order to determine the demand for entrepreneurs, we must consider the supply of entrepreneurial capacities. Hence, to start with we have to raise the question, what is it that entrepreneurs do?

Basically entrepreneurs operate between markets. But they also transform entities obtained in one market into entities sold in another. Hence, entrepreneurs must be able to perceive (1) buying and selling opportunities in different markets, (2) the possibility of transforming inputs into outputs, and (3) determine that activities (1) and (2) will be profitable. These perceptions may be based on existing inputs, existing outputs, and existing transformation procedures or on innovations in some or all of these categories. This puts the matter very abstractly. For instance, access to finance may be critical in making the other aspects possible, but access to finance is unlikely to be sufficient. If the requisite activities cannot be carried out profitably, a going concern will not be created. Furthermore, we have already argued that where markets are perfect, the ability to trade between markets and to transform inputs into outputs becomes a trivial ability since the technical skill of transforming inputs into outputs is also something purchasable in the marketplace. Hence, we have to restrict our attention to markets and contexts in which imperfections exist.

While there is a wide variety of things entrepreneurship may be concerned with, from our point of view, we may focus on two essential aspects. The entrepreneur is (1) a *gap filler* and (2) an *input completer*. Both of these activities arise from the basic assumptions of X-efficiency theory. If not all factors of production are marketed or if there are imperfections in markets, the entrepreneur has to fill the gaps in the market. In other words, any input that is not readily available on equal terms to all buyers or to all potential buyers must somehow be marshaled by the entrepreneur. Further, it is not sufficient that only *some* of the market gaps be filled or *some* of the imperfections be overcome. It is in fact critical that enough of the gaps be filled and enough of the imperfections overcome so that the enterprise can be put in motion, as it were, and kept in motion. Hence the nature of the entrepreneurial activities depends simultaneously on the nature of and the variety of markets necessary to launch a firm and keep it going. The more imperfect the markets, the greater the entrepreneurial skills required.

WHAT DOES THE ENTREPRENEUR GET?

Given that the entrepreneur has to possess the unusual skills of being a gap filler and an input completer, what does he get for using these skills? Where imperfect markets are involved the return is more than simply pure profits. In addition the entrepreneur or entrepreneurs could expect indirect pecuniary gains as well as a variety of nonpecuniary advantages. The entrepreneur is not only the possible residual claimant after expenses are paid, but he also has the authority that is inherent to owners or to major stockholders. This is especially the case where relatively small businesses are involved. Among the indirect pecuniary advantages is that the owner can employ himself and members of his family in positions which may be superior to what he or they could find elsewhere as employees. He has a foothold in an enterprise which could possibly expand and grow large if things go well. Thus in a sense he is also the purchaser of a lottery ticket which would allow him to become much wealthier and which he would not possess were he simply an employee or a small minority investor in a very large enterprise. Finally, among the nonpecuniary advantages is that (to a degree) he can set his own conditions of work for himself as well as for those members of his family. While part of the challenge of entrepreneurship is to overcome market imperfections, if he is successful he obtains the advantage of controlling an enterprise in an imperfect market. In addition the market imperfections may allow him to raise prices in response to inflationary pressures and hence operate as a hedge against inflation.

Of course the advantages we have mentioned will depend on the specific circumstances in which the entrepreneur finds himself, the size of the firm, and the nature of the market. Nevertheless these indirect pecuniary advantages as well as the nonpecuniary ones must be considered as powerful incentives in addition to the pure profit incentive which would exist in perfectly competitive markets.

Much of the above discussion involves examples of a more general set of ideas. The potential pecuniary and nonpecuniary gains are a consequence of the entrepreneur's inherent capacity to determine the residual rights and responsibilities for the firm. In other words, many of the arrangements made by the entrepreneur will involve implicit contractual arrangements which will not exhaust either the gross revenue of the enterprise or other rights and responsibilities that exist in the running of the enterprise. As a consequence the entrepreneur is likely to be a residual claimant not only to the income of the enterprise but also to whatever residual authority and responsibility exists after all other contracts are determined. In some cases the entrepreneur may "contract away" many residual claims to others, e.g., common stock holders, but in any event he is likely to be in a powerful position to arrange the distribution of residual claims and responsibilities. In short, as the input completer, the entrepreneur is in a critical position to work out favorable contractual arrangements for himself. It would be incorrect to argue that the entrepreneur is necessarily the residual claimant. He may be the residual claimant or he may "sell" that right for another form of remuneration.

THE DEMAND FOR ENTREPRENEURSHIP—

THE INTERACTION OF OPPORTUNITIES AND CAPACITIES

We have seen that demand for entrepreneurship depends on two elements: (1) the supply of economic opportunities and (2) the potential supply of entrepreneurial capacities. We will now consider these matters in greater detail.

We may visualize an entrepreneurial opportunity set composed of two subsets. The first subset involves the techniques currently in use within the economy and the use of inputs which are relatively well marketed. In this subset we would expect a new entrepreneur to engage in similar activities to those already in the industry in question. The mere fact that techniques are already in use does *not* imply that new firms cannot be started by using the same techniques. Probably most entrepreneurial activities do not involve innovative techniques to any considerable degree, but rather involve coping with the methods of doing business and of combining inputs quite similar to those combinations already in existence. This is the province of the conventional entrepreneur.

The other subset of the entrepreneurial opportunity set involves techniques not in use in the economy. We may start with the concept of all the possible production possibilities in the sense that they involve knowledge conceivably attainable from somewhere at some cost. These production possibilities may be obtainable within the economy in question or outside. Thus, if an entrepreneur were to make a significant search for some technique and after such a search would be able to find it, we would consider such a technique as belonging to this subset. This would include techniques that could only be adopted by unusual entrepreneurs who could overcome gaps in the market, imperfections in the market, or other obstacles. The opportunities may be said to exist whether or not the economy contains the kind of entrepreneurs capable of taking advantage of these opportunities. By definition this part of the entrepreneurial opportunity set would attract only innovating entrepreneurs.

By recalling our discussion of two topics, we can readily see the essential elements involved in the demand for entrepreneurship. On the one hand we have to keep in mind the nature of the economy which provides through its holes, gaps, obstacles in the pathway of inputs and existing inefficiencies a quantum of potential entrepreneurial opportunities. In other words it is the supply of gaps and obstacles that could conceivably be overcome that provides the entrepreneurial opportunities in the system. But the opportunities are not meaningful unless there exist individuals in the economy who could be the gap fillers and input completers and who could take advantage of the opportunity. Thus the supply of simultaneous gap filling and input completing skills is the other element that determines the demand for existing entrepreneurial talents. Whether or not these talents are used will depend on the entrepreneur's motivational setting which will determine the supply of entrepreneurship actually forthcoming.

THE SUPPLY OF ENTREPRENEURSHIP

The supply side is determined by the following: the set of individuals with gap-filling and input-completing capacities, the sociocultural and political constraints which influence the extent to which enterpreneurs take advantage of their capacities, and the degree to which potential entrepreneurs respond to different motivational states, especially where nontraditional activities are involved. Clearly the personality characteristics of entrepreneurs are important. Apart from gap-filling and input-completing capacities, the potential entrepreneur's response to opportunities will depend on his preference for certain modes of behavior as opposed to others.

Only those individuals who have the necessary skills to perceive entrepreneurial opportunities, to carry out the required input gap-filling activities, and to be *input-completers* can be potential entrepreneurs. In addition, whether or not an individual will use his entrepreneurial skills will depend on the utility he receives from entrepreneurial profits and entrepreneurial activities compared to the utility he receives from other modes of producing income. In many cases only a small proportion of those with entrepreneurial capacities will actually be available to carry out entrepreneurial activities.

The crucial aspect about the supply of entrepreneurship is that only in fairly rare cases is it a completely generalized skill. In other words, the capacity to take advantage of opportunities will generally be limited to a specific industry or to a small set of industries, and to specific locals. Returning to the entrepreneurial opportunity set, we should visualize the demand and supply as being segmented and applicable to a very large number of subsets in the opportunity set. Indeed, for many subsets in the opportunity set, there may be no potential entrepreneurs whatsoever.

It is also worth noting that the gap-filling opportunity set is not likely to be unique since the costs associated with gap-filling depend on the specific entrepreneur who attempts to take advantage of the opportunity. The sequence in which gap-fillers choose opportunities will determine the degree to which any one opportunity turns out to be profitable. In addition, the degree of effort put forth by different entrepreneurs and the same entrepreneur at different times will vary, depending on the personality, circumstances, and the motivating influences that exist at the time. Thus, the association between gap-filling opportunities and profitable opportunities is not likely to be a unique one-to-one correspondence.

CONSEQUENCES AND APPLICATIONS

A significant distinction has to be made between conventional entrepreneurs and innovating entrepreneurs. The conventional entrepreneur enters a market that already exists at more or less the conventional scale and producing the commodity or service in the conventional way. Whether something is conventional or not depends on the technology in use and practices in a given economy. Can we have a surplus of conventional entrepreneurs? There is a sense in which this is possible, although it is very difficult to assess the importance of the possibility.

Consider the case in which there are shops for a certain product in relatively small towns, spaced relatively far apart. Is it better to have fewer or more shops of this kind? In part this depends on the pricing system which these shops will employ. Suppose they use what they believe to be normal profit rate target prices. Now consider the case of three versus four shops. They compete for a fixed market and, let us assume, for a product with a relatively inelastic demand. In the case of three shops each shares approximately a third of the market whereas in the case of four shops they share a quarter of the market. The investment is approximately the same under the two alternatives, and hence the price is somewhat higher in the four shop case in order to yield the same profit level. Clearly there is more excess capacity in the four shop case and what we may interpret as a greater degree of X-inefficiency. There exists the possibility that a surplus of conventional entrepreneurs in the village can lead to the four shop case being the operative one, if the alternatives for the family workers in the four shop case would be a much lower level of consumption as outside employees. Obviously the four shop case is surrounded by a number of very special assumptions. The extent to which they are likely to hold will depend on specific circumstances and the nature of specific markets. Nevertheless, in analyzing development problems this case cannot be ignored, although it may be relatively unimportant in the long run.

Under long-run circumstances we would expect enough internal migration and opportunities for small entrepreneurs as well as expanding entrepreneural skills and horizons so that additional entrepreneurial capacities would increase rather than decrease X-efficiency.

POLICY IMPLICATIONS AND CONCLUSIONS

The supply of entrepreneurship in any industry influences the degree of X-inefficiency in that industry. We can visualize a supply of entrepreneurship curve (see figure 3.1) which relates the cost of producing a product and the possibility of entrepreneurs increasing the (net) capacity of the industry. At some cost there will be zero new capacity created. As cost rises more entrepreneurs find it easier to marshal the resources to enter the industry and to create new capacity. The main point to note is that there may be *no* additional entrepreneurship at a cost well above minimal cost possible. It would seem self evident that the capacity for entrepreneurs to enter and to organize new firms at some given cost will determine the degree of X-inefficiency in the industry.

We emphasized three elements as determining the actual employment of entrepreneurial skills. Those were (1) the supply of economic opportunities, (2) the supply of entrepreneurial

Figure 3.1

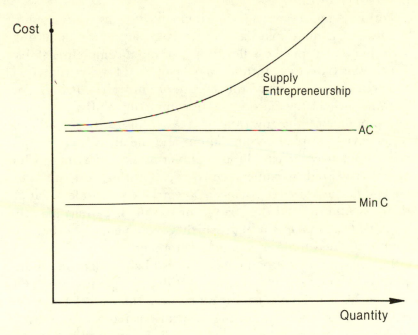

AC = Average cost
Min C = Minimum possible cost, i.e., zero X-inefficiency

skills or capacity, and (3) the supply of entrepreneurship itself. The last component, the supply of entrepreneurship, depends on alternative opportunities available to potential entrepreneurs, as well as on the value society places on entrepreneurship as an activity versus the alternative occupations available to the entrepreneurs. In some cases employment in the civil service, the professions, political careers, careers in church organizations, military organizations may carry greater prestige than entrepreneurship, and this will influence the supply. While the supply of entrepreneurial opportunities is likely to change as given opportunities are filled and new ones arise as a consequence, the supply of entrepreneurial skills and of entrepreneurship is likely to change much more slowly in a society. It is the latter two components that are likely to influence the rate of income growth.

For purposes of economic development it seems reasonable to presume that there may be a fairly large supply of gap-filling skills but a very much smaller supply of input-completing skills. Where this is the case, avenues may be opened for governmental intervention to influence the supply of entrepreneurship. For example, where the missing input-completing skill is the provision of finance, the government creation of institutions which foster savings, capital accumulation, and the allocation of capital to users may increase input-completing skills for those who are currently only gap-fillers. Of course, how this works out will depend on specific circumstances. Nevertheless, consideration of these possibilities and the analysis of specific situations may reveal fruitful sources through which governments or other organizations may foster economic development.

In a general sense economic growth is likely to depend on the supply of cost reducing and innovating entrepreneurship. Of course these are not separate categories. Innovative entrepreneurs who have the capacity to start firms, or reorganize existing firms, which reduces the level of X-inefficiency, are likely to be the ones to contribute significantly to economic development.

On the whole we have considered entrepreneurship from a conceptual viewpoint. In later chapters we shall use the concept of entrepreneurship developed in this chapter and augmented by other concepts in order to help us analyze general problems that arise in the course of economic development.

4 | Agricultural Surplus Labor

BACKGROUND AND REVIEW OF EXISTING LITERATURE

One of the oldest controversies in development economics is that which surrounds the concept of disguised unemployment in the agricultural sector of "less developed" countries (LDCs). This concept plays a prominent role in the work of Rosenstein-Rodan, Nurske, Lewis, and others,[1] who are among the early pioneers in the development field. The issues are quite clearly brought out in the early debate between Nurske and Jacob Viner.[2] The controversy, both theoretical and empirical is best summarized by Warren Robinson as follows:

Disguised unemployment has come in for a considerable amount of discussion, pro and con, since Rosenstein-Rodan and later Nurske first made it part of their explanations of economic backwardness. The notion has been developed rather exhaustively at the theoretical level, especially as it applies to agriculture, and W. Arthur Lewis and Fei and Ranis have con-

[1] Ragnar Nurske, *Problems of Capital Formation in Lesser Developed Areas* (Oxford: Oxford University Press, 1955); W. Arthur Lewis, "Economic Development with Unlimited Supplies of Labour," *Manchester School*, May 1954; P. N. Rosenstein-Rodan, "Disguised Unemployment and Underemployment in Agriculture," *Monthly Bulletin of Agricultural Economics and Statistics* (FAO) 6 (1957).
[2] J. Viner, "On the Concept of Disguised Unemployment," *Indiana Journal of Economics*, July 1957.

56

structed elaborate models in which the concept is assigned a key role. Empirical studies, aimed at measuring the extent of the "surplus" labour which the disguised unemployment represents, have also been attempted but the results have been, to say the least, rather more unclear. Kao, Anschel, and Eicher, reviewing some of the more important of the empirical studies, concluded: "To date, there is little reliable evidence to support the existence of more than token—5 per cent—disguised unemployment in underdeveloped countries." But, Yong Sam Cho's very careful investigation of South Korean agriculture reaches an opposite conclusion: ". . . approximately 30 per cent of the total labour time available annually is unutilized." In the case of India, there is an even more direct conflict of research findings. Mathur concluded that: "In West Bengal, which is one of the most thickly populated states of India, disguised unemployment comes out to be almost one-third (33.1 per cent) of the rural working force." On the other hand, on the basis of studying the data of the Indian Farm Management Institute, Paglin concluded that the marginal product of labour in Indian agriculture is positive and that there is no substantial amount of surplus labour. Thus, the empirical results are contradictory and one is at a loss to understand why.[3]

The general view of those who believe in disguised unemployment is roughly as follows. The agricultural sectors of many developing countries are densely populated. Studies by agronomists and others suggest that the output of the agricultural sector could be produced by less individuals than those currently living on or employed in that sector. Hence, from this point of view a surplus of labor exists.[4] According to Nurske this surplus should be viewed as an advantage rather than a disadvantage. It represents a resource that could be used elsewhere in the economy in order to develop economies with generally scarce re-

[3] Warren C. Robinson, "Types of Disguised Rural Unemployment and Some Policy Implications," *Oxford Economic Papers* 21, no. 3 (November 1969):373; he also provides a detailed bibliography on the subject. Another excellent bibliography exists in A. K. Sen, *Employment, Technology, and Development* (Oxford: Clarendon Press, 1975). Sen's book is worth referring to on the issues discussed in this chapter as well as those questions which involve the problem of dualism and the choice of technology.

[4] See W. E. Moore, *Economic Demography of Eastern and Southern Europe* (Geneva: League of Nations Publications, 1944) and Doreen Warriner, *Economics of Peasant Farming* (Oxford: Oxford University Press, 1939).

sources.[5] Thus, the lack of capital can be substituted for by the essentially free labor that exists in economies of this sort. Part of the vision behind this viewpoint is the shift of labor from the agricultural to other sectors and the use of this "free" labor for the production of capital goods to foster economic development. Since these migrants represent surplus labor, then by definition those left on the land could produce (with fewer people) the same amount of food that was produced before by more individuals. The surplus food created in this way in the agricultural area could be shipped to the other sectors to feed the migrants from the agricultural area. While one could quibble about the additional transport resources involved or the fact that in order to produce capital goods, other capital goods are required in addition to the previously surplus labor, these are essentially quibbles. The point remains that if a significant amount of surplus labor exists, then with proper organization this can operate as a resource to foster development. The opposition to this view has been argued on two bases: (1) an empirical one and (2) a theoretical one. The theoretical issues are of most interest because they give the impression that the surplus labor of the type considered cannot exist under the stated or presumed conditions *even as a possibility*.

The theoretical difficulty rests on the fact that there exists an actual or implicit positive wage in the agricultural sector. It is argued that if the wage is positive, then the value of the marginal product of labor must also be positive. As a consequence, if such labor is removed, the marginal product that it previously created is also removed thereby, and, as a result, the smaller labor force cannot possibly produce the same output as was formerly produced with the larger labor force if nonlabor inputs are kept constant. Thus, those who believe in the workability of markets in the agricultural sector could not give any possible credence to the view that surplus labor could exist where agri-

5 Nurske, op. cit.

cultural workers were actually or implicitly receiving a positive wage.

Agricultural workers receive a positive wage where agriculture is organized in terms of landless laborers working for land owners. Therefore, in the case of share cropping, family members who work the land earn an income from their effort which is positive and which could not be lower than the alternative wage for landless laborers. The same would hold for small holders using only or mostly family labor. Thus it was argued as long as an agricultural market exists to some degree, and as long as those employed as family workers could, in principal, choose to work in the wage labor market, then a positive wage, actual or implicit, is inconsistent with the concept of disguised unemployment. Economists such as Jacob Viner, and later T. W. Schultz argued that while the marginal productivity of agricultural labor may be quite low, it is not zero and hence surplus labor does not exist. Although a number of other issues were brought into the discussion, this is the basic argument that emerged from the application of standard micro-economic theory to this particular problem.

Now, we must separate two questions; the empirical and the theoretical. Whether or not surplus labor exists in some specific country or in a portion of a country is an empirical question. We can use theory to argue whether or not the presumed measurements are appropriate, but we cannot argue what the measurements would show, without actually making measurements, from a purely theoretical viewpoint. Thus, in this chapter, we will consider whether it is possible to have a positive wage rate and to have simultaneously the existence of surplus labor.

Parenthetically we should note that one cannot argue that because a positive wage rate exists, that surplus labor does not exist, in some specific instance and country. One may perhaps argue that it would be reasonable to expect that surplus labor would not exist, but not that it is factually so. The reason for this is that if measurements disclosed that surplus labor did indeed exist, we might have an anomalous set of facts that could not otherwise be explained; the measurements and their results would have to determine the existence of or lack of surplus labor. In other words, just as one cannot show, on theoretical grounds, that surplus labor exists in some specific country, so one cannot show, by the existence of a positive wage, that surplus labor does not exist.

THE BASIC PRODUCTIVITY-EFFORT MODEL

It is surprising that very little of the writing involved in this controversy includes effort as an explicit *discretionary* variable. Once we do so we can see that many aspects that appear simultaneously contradictory need not be. This is especially true of the possibility of a positive implicit wage (or explicit wage) and of the existence of surplus labor in the sense of Nurske and Lewis. The following artificial example includes most of the elements it is necessary to consider, and yet strips the problem to its essentials so that we can judge what variations of the assumptions are necessary to obtain various types of conclusions.

We consider an agricultural sector made up of uniform plots of land of equal size and quality on which, in the initial stage (situation *A*), five people work each plot. (1) Each plot is a family farm. (2) The rent is paid for by those working it, and it is the same for each plot. (3) Under any given set of circumstances each worker works at the same pace and the same effort level as every other worker; and (4) the degree of effort depends on the number of people working the land. (5) All workers are identical.

Consider in particular the special case in which effort increases in direct proportion to the decrease in the number of individuals in a given plot of land. Now suppose that one-fifth of the laborers migrate to the urban sector. Suppose further that this occurs through one member of every farm leaving so that four of the previous five remain to do the work. If the four that are left put forth twenty-five percent more effort, these four individuals will do as much work as was previously performed by five. This implies that effort is shared equally for the work to be done whether there are five or four individuals to do the work involved. It is effort that produced the output and not the number of workers. Hence if the aggregate effort is the same with four workers per farm as was previously the case with five then output should be the same. While the assumptions were made to insure a particular result, it is undeniable that this scenario is possible.

Now let us compare situation A (the five worker per farm situation) with situation B (the four worker per farm) in terms of wage rates, marginal productivities, etc. It is clear that the productivity per person under A is smaller than the productivity under B. Furthermore the implicit wage rate under A is equal to the average wage rate and is also equal to the marginal wage rate. Thus the value of the marginal product would in fact be equal to the wage both in situation A and in situation B. However, the wage rate under B would be 1.25 times the wage rate under A. Thus in this case under both situations A and B we would have a positive wage rate and a positive value of the marginal product of labor. However, while the value of the marginal product of labor is in terms of the "usual" assumptions, we shall see that it is nevertheless a special assumption.

The marginal product per *man* really has no specific meaning unless we indicate how we treat effort. The usual assumption is that effort is presumed to remain the same as we consider more or less workers. From this viewpoint the wage is equal to the value of the marginal product, and the marginal product is positive in both cases.

Is there an anomaly about a positive wage and a zero marginal product? From a macro viewpoint we note that as we shift from A to B there is no loss of aggregate output despite the fact that twenty percent of the labor force has been removed from the land. From this point of view we can argue that there is at least twenty percent surplus labor as we shift from situation A

to situation *B*. Thus, in this sense surplus labor and a positive wage rate are perfectly consistent with each other. There is also a sense in which, as we have argued before, the notion that the wage rate is equal to the value of the marginal product is not vitiated.

Is there a sense in which the marginal productivity of labor may be said to equal zero? In the particular case under discussion, we might say that the marginal product of labor for a *given effort level* is positive, but that the marginal product of labor for the changing effort levels as we shift from *A* to *B* is zero. However, it can be argued that the appropriate concept of marginal productivity that determines the wage rate is marginal product demand for a given effort level. Hence the wage being equal to the value of the marginal product is consistent with this example. In other words, a given set of institutional arrangements will imply a given effort level for workers, *on the average*. When we compare situations *A* and *B*, we are really comparing alternative institutional arrangements and alternative supplies of labor which are inappropriate to determine the wage rate at any specific time. The marginal productivity of labor as a consequence of migration is a different concept than the marginal productivity of labor for the same supply of labor. Once we make effort a variable all of this is quite clear and what previously appeared as an anomaly is now demystified.

We now contrast the variable effort model with the conventional assumptions. Since the conventional theory does not say anything about effort, it is impossible to know what assumption is really implicit in the conventional theory. An assumption consistent with the theory would be one in which effort per man is fixed. The contrast between this assumption and the previous model is fairly straightforward. If we shift from situation *A* to situation *B*, in which there are less workers, then on the basis of the assumption just made, we must obtain proportionately less aggregate effort, and we would normally expect less aggregate output. (Except in those cases where the marginal productivity of effort is zero.) If the marginal productivity of effort is not zero, then we must expect that less will be produced in situation *B*, and hence we would argue that no surplus labor can exist under these circumstances. What we see clearly is that the introduction of effort as a variable does not imply the necessary absence of surplus labor, whereas if effort is fixed then surplus labor could exist only if the marginal productivity of effort is zero.

Under what circumstances would we expect effort to be a variable? In my view this would be a variable in almost all cases. The two exceptions are those in which there is a fixed and determinate wage contract at the outset or in which labor is working at the maximum effort level. We will consider both later. In the meantime it would be useful to consider some examples in which effort is a variable.

In a previous analysis of this problem (1957), I presented a special case of the above model in which food and effort are connected. According to this model, in low food consumption per capita countries, an improvement in nutrition would be translated into an improvement in overall strength and health and hence an increase in the effort level. The results for the specific cases are of course quite similar to the more general case which we wish to consider here. I now believe this case is partially deficient since it does not consider motivational elements. It is one thing to suggest that food increases strength and it is something else to suggest that the increased effort capacity will in fact be used. Nevertheless the implicit assumption is that effort capacity would be used, and hence we obtain a model similar to the more general case considered here. In addition to food we might consider other elements, especially those related to health, including those that involve psychological well being, which would increase effort capacity per capita.

It seems self-evident that effort is rarely, if ever, at a maximum. If that is the case then the amount of effort would depend on individual motivation and especially on that aspect of individual motivation related to interpersonal relationships. In such interpersonal relationships some of which are peer relations and some vertical relationships, the amount of effort put forth depends on established institutional arrangements within working groups. Of special interest is the case of family farms. In this case we would expect a certain amount of effort sharing, though the age and sex distributions of family members would have to be taken into account. If we assume that, in the short run, there is an amount of targeted work to be done then we would normally expect that for the same target more family members would involve less effort being put forth per person. Thus as family members move off the farm, effort levels would gradually increase. Whether the increased effort is translated into more hours of work, more rapid pace levels, more efficient ways of doing things, or some combination of all three would depend on particular circumstances. In general, we should expect that all three types of changes would take place.

Outside of the family as the working context, we should expect "conventional" effort standards to be developed. Such a standard would be relatively fixed in the short run but would shift in the longer run with changes in supply of labor and possibly with the wage rate. How such standards are established in detail and how they change in time is an uninvestigated subject. What is clear from the literature of labor economics is that effort standards are developed and furthermore that they vary considerably over time and space. A scarcity of labor in a situation may involve a very different effort standard than one in which there is considerable unemployment. The motivational context of the two cases are different and hence the effort put forth is also different. The implication of conventional standards, which shift in the long run, is that effort is not fully utilized and furthermore that effort changes with time. The circumstances surrounding the determination of specific effort conventions are likely to depend in part on past history, the relative supply of labor, and the availability of other inputs.

THE PEAK LABOR DEMAND ARGUMENT

One of the main arguments that has been put forth against surplus labor proponents is that the nature of agriculture requires great seasonal variations in labor demand. Hence, to the extent that there appears to be underutilized labor, it is in the offseason. During the peak demand period, all of the labor available is required. As a statement about some specific empirical situation, it may very well be true, but it is difficult to see that this should necessarily be generally true or exactly what it means with respect to the possibility of surplus labor.

We shall not be concerned here with the question of seasonal unemployment except as it may have bearing on the problem of general unemployment. Seasonably underutilized labor is of course an almost ubiquitous phenomenon in agriculture in LDCs. How to harness this source of labor power presents some special problems worthy of consideration. However, this is not the place to deviate from our main concern which is the possible existence of surplus labor apart from the seasonal components. The existence of seasonal unemployment does not seem to have been a subject of controversy; it is generally recognized to exist.

The main burden of the seasonal demand argument is that the seasonal peak demand for agricultural labor determines the aggregate demand for labor. Thus, if there is no surplus labor in the peak season then surplus labor does not exist. This essentially was one of the early arguments presented by Harry Oshima.[6]

In Oshima's argument, effort (in our sense) does not appear explicitly as a variable. Hence it is difficult to say what the implicit effort assumption is presumed to be. In a more refined analysis which was presented by Stiglitz, the effort variable is

[6] H. T. Oshima, "Unemployment in Backward Economies: an Empirical Comment," *Journal of Political Economy* 66 (1958).

made somewhat more explicit. Stiglitz assumes that in the peak season ". . . laborers are assumed to be fully utilized (i.e., *work the maximum that is possible at those times*), and the other times of the year, . . . the supply of labor (hours worked per week) by each laborer is determined so as to maximize utility."[7]

We should note that in terms of the language developed earlier Stiglitz assumes that maximum effort is put forth during the peak season and that there is no substitution in any direction. It is also important to consider that to the extent that an effort concept is implicitly involved it is basically in terms of numbers of hours of work. For the most part the components of pace, quality of the effort, or the nature of the detailed activities involved are never used. It is perhaps not too hard to conceive of effort being a maximum if we see it only in terms of *hours* of work. It may be more difficult if we consider the other components. Thus there are two elements involved in this analysis: what is meant by maximum effort? and is it likely to really exist in this case?

If maximum effort is in fact put forth and the maximum implies maximum output, then of course, the argument of Oshima, Stiglitz, and others would, in fact, be true. Under this assumption there would be no surplus labor. But the assumption does not follow from the mere fact that agricultural labor is seasonal in nature. The maximum effort, maximum productivity, no substitutions assumptions are in addition to the fact of the seasonal nature of labor demand.

It does not take much reflection to realize that one could have seasonal demand for labor and still have the possibility of surplus labor. The first and most obvious possibility is the case in which the peak season does not require maximum effort by all or by most workers. What is observable is not *maximum* effort

[7] J. E. Stiglitz, "Alternative Theory of Wage Determination and Unemployment in LDC's: I. The Labor Turnover Model," Cowles Foundation Discussion Paper No. 335, 1972, Yale University, New Haven.

•

but the fact that considerably *greater* effort is put forth during the peak season than in the off-season. Whether or not the greater effort implies maximum effort is a completely different matter. Whatever the empirical case may be in most instances, in principle it is certainly possible for the greater amount of effort not to be equal to the maximum effort, and hence for surplus labor to exist in the sense in which the term has been used previously. In other words, after labor is removed from the land, there is a reallocation of duties and of pace within duties, so that we end up with more effort per man, more output per man, and the increased output being equal to what it was prior to the labor having left the land.

A second possibility, even if effort was at a maximum initially, is substitution over time as well as possible substitution in other directions. If there is enough manpower it may be thought desirable to minimize the number of days in which the harvesting takes place. But with less manpower it may be possible to increase the number of harvesting days without decreasing production to any extent. What is important to consider is the possibility that flexibility exists with respect to harvesting time and/or with respect to other directions that determine production. Thus, even if extending the harvesting period may result in some loss of output, other things equal, there may be other areas within which a change of effort would make up that loss. In part adjustments could be made by changing the mix of crops in accordance with requiring a somewhat lengthier harvest time, the type of seeds used, the type of equipment employed, and the organization of labor. Thus, it may be possible that a variety of changes in effort may yield the same output with a lesser number of workers than with more.

What are likely to be the facts in this situation? In the absence of empirical studies within which effort in our sense is a basic variable, we can only speculate about likelihoods. It seems likely that the amount of effort in the peak season, in our sense (and not in the number of hours sense), is not a maximum in all instances. Thus, the mere fact that the hours worked are considerably greater in the peak season should not lead to the inference that maximum effort is put forth. In fact, it seems unlikely that in many instances there would not be the possibility for increasing effort for a portion of the labor force if workers are withdrawn. To the extent that this exists, it may be possible to increase aggregate effort by substituting greater effort workers after the shift, for those who produced less effort and left the agricultural sector. In other words, it seems unlikely that there should not be some possible changes in the components of effort so that a smaller population should enable us to increase productivity.

A point to be noted is that in the Stiglitz paper the assumption is made that maximum effort implies maximum marginal output from the worker involved during the peak season. But that is because effort is viewed, or is implicitly assumed to contain, a single dimension. In a multidimensional conception of effort, it is possible to have a number of maximum effort levels in the sense of possible degrees of felt effortfulness, each level associated with different amounts of productivity. If, in addition, the effort vector is connected with the number of people doing the work, it is possible for a maximum effort level with fewer workers to yield the same amount of output as a different maximum effort level associated with more workers. In other words, during the peak season, peer group pressures and the interpersonal standard of fairness require that everyone appear to work at a maximum level. But with fewer people they work at the same degree of apparent effortfulness, do somewhat different things, and produce the same amount as was produced with more workers.

THE UTILITY OF WORK AS A CONSIDERATION

Thus far in our discussion we did not take into account the utility of labor in determining the supply of labor. In the conven-

tional analysis it is usually assumed that workers choose between the value of labor versus the value of leisure. The utility
of labor is assumed to be equivalent to the wage the worker receives for his work. As a result the number of hours worked is
determined by the point at which the wage rate is just equal to
the utility of the marginal hour of leisure. This type of analysis
does add one additional consideration to the problem, namely,
it is one thing to argue that workers could produce more if there
was more work to be done, so to speak, and it is another thing to
argue that they would in fact wish to do so. Thus, reducing the
labor force by twenty percent may provide twenty percent more
work to do and workers may indeed have the time to do it, but
they may not choose to do so.

Let us proceed with our previous example and apply the utility of labor to the utility of leisure analysis. Suppose as before
that twenty percent of the population leaves the agricultural labor force. There is indeed more work to do. Let us assume that
people can work more hours. They currently work an eight-
hour day, they can increase labor time to a ten-hour day, and,
with equal productivity per hour as an assumption, they can
produce as much in ten hours with the smaller labor force as
the larger one produced in eight. Would they choose to work
ten hours? Let us assume for a moment that the marginal productivity per worker is constant per hour both under the old arrangements prior to the migration and under the new arrangements. If the marginal productivity is the same as before and
hence the wage is the same as before, then the new equilibrium
number of hours should also be the same as before. Thus workers would work only eight hours and no additional output
would be forthcoming. If on the other hand we make the reasonable assumption that with fewer workers the marginal productivity of labor rises, although it falls with increasing hours
of work, then with twenty percent less labor we should expect a
higher product for the marginal hour. Therefore, workers
should be induced to work more than eight hours because the

return is now greater than the marginal utility of an hour of leisure.

Nevertheless, workers would not wish to work the full ten hours to make up for all the labor hours lost by those who migrated. This can be readily seen; if labor worked ten hours, the productivity for the marginal hour is the same as it was with more workers and an eight-hour day, but the utility value of the previous hours of leisure must be higher under a ten-hour day. Hence, workers might work say, a nine-hour day and make up for some of the productivity lost due to migration but not for all of it.

But the conventional leisure/work trade-off analysis may not be the appropriate one. If we introduce the concept of interpersonal determinants of utility for both the utility of work and the utility of leisure and if we introduce the other components involved in effort, we can obtain somewhat different results. Let us look at the problem in terms of pace. The advantage of looking at it in terms of pace is that we do not necessarily cut into hours of leisure when there is more work to be done. In other words it may be possible to increase output entirely by increasing pace or by changing other components of effort without affecting hours of work. Let us also introduce the concept of the inert area. We can now suppose that everyone's effort position prior to migration was in their inert areas. Migration results in a reshuffling of the tasks among individuals, and they now have to work at an increased pace. This may bring everyone into a new inert area. What is not at all clear is what happens to utility under these circumstances. If at the old pace level the utility was on the average lower than the maximum then the higher pace increases utility up to a point. However, we must keep in mind that the interpersonal relationships are likely to change the shape of the effort-utility relationship. Thus under the new amount of effort and the changed effort-utility relationship, workers may feel that they are at no lower utility level than they were prior to the changeover.

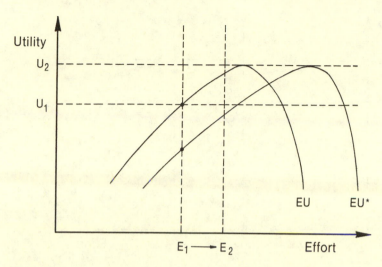

Figure 4.1

The above ideas will be illustrated and discussed briefly with the aid of figures 4.1 and 4.2. In both diagrams U_1U_2 represents the initial inert area. In figure 4.1 the relation marked *EU* is the relation between effort and utility prior to the migration of labor. The relation marked *EU** represents the same relationship *after* the migration takes place. The labels *EU* and *EU** should be interpreted in a similar manner in figure 4.2. The effort level prior to migration is designated by E_1. We observe in figure 4.1 that the relation shift from *EU* to *EU** causes the initial effort position to fall outside the inert area. As a result we now have a motivation for individuals to shift from effort position E_1 to a greater effort position E_2. In figure 4.2 we illustrate the situation in which the initial effort position is beyond maximum utility. Similar to figure 4.1, in figure 4.2 the initial effort position falls outside of the inert area after migration and this induces a shift towards E_2. How far effort shifts depends on the process of movement and at what points people discover the actual utility of a higher effort position. For present purposes it is

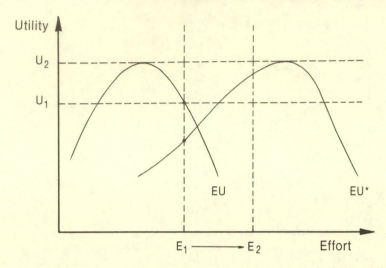

Figure 4.2

not important whether the shift is all the way so as to achieve the maximum utility level associated with effort, or whether the process takes place in steps so that inertia as a force enters at some point and the new effort E_2 position falls short of the one associated with maximal utility.

Basically the figures describe the influence of vertical and horizontal pressures on the individual within the changed situation so that the new utility level for the old effort level falls and at the same time increases the effort level compared to what it would have been with the old manpower per farm. The figures suggest the possibility of increased effort being generated as a consequence of withdrawing labor from the agricultural sector, but of course it by no means establishes that this will necessarily happen.

THE CASE OF EMPLOYED LABOR

In the previous discussion we assumed that labor was self-employed as it were. We were either discussing a system of family farms or a system of families renting farms on a share-cropping basis. The utilization of labor in which the workers are landless involves some slightly different analytical features. Nevertheless we will want to argue that even in this case it will follow that farm owners may pay a positive wage and yet at the same time we can have an equilibrium consistent with the concept of surplus labor.

In the conventional view effort does not enter explicitly as a variable. If there is surplus labor then this would imply that there would be visible unemployment. Furthermore, the unemployed would drive the wage down to a point where the marginal product exceeded the wage so that more would be employed. The marginal product could not be zero since this would imply a zero wage for the employed workers. However, on the basis of the arguments used previously, we shall see that this need not be the case.

To start with consider the case of disguised unemployment. Suppose there is a conventional standard of effort designated by E_1. We further suppose that at the effort level E_1 all workers are employed. We can then visualize a twenty percent migration out of agriculture and an eventual shift to a higher effort level equal to E_2 which would be equal to $1.25\ E_1$. But let us return to our consideration of the initial lower effort level E_1. What could determine such an effort level? We use the word conventional standard to hint at what is involved. In terms of the ideas presented in chapter two, we can visualize the standard as determined by a balance of vertical and horizontal pressures, which eventually are within the inert areas of the individuals involved. Essentially we visualize peer group pressures (horizontal) as being towards lower effort levels and the employer-management pressures (vertical) as being towards higher levels. Given the standard it is easy to visualize an effort level implying a marginal product equal to the wage at the conventional standard of E_1. Through some sort of a process, as the one illustrated and discussed in connections with figures 4.1 and 4.2, we can visualize a shift in the effort standards for the average employee towards E_2. Thus, from this viewpoint no serious difficulty arises in obtaining our results within the context of employed landless laborers.

We now consider the case of *visible* unemployment. In a sense the case of visible unemployment is simpler than that of disguised unemployment. As long as the unemployed are the ones who migrate, there is no difficulty in seeing that the existing labor force can produce as much as before. The only question which arises is why unemployment should be consistent with a positive wage rate. Why should the unemployed not drive wages down so that full employment emerges? In part this may be similar to the Keynesian problem for developed economies. But these are not the arguments we shall stress here.

The basic argument is that an effort equilibrium can exist simultaneously with visible unemployment. On the one hand the unemployed may want a "fair wage" for employment—which they may interpret to be the going wage. On the other hand employers may find it difficult to offer a lower wage, even if it were accepted, since this would involve either offering discriminatory wages, which would appear threatening to other workers, or the employer would have to recontract with existing workers. Recontracting towards a lower wage may not be feasible or practical since employees can respond by producing less effort. Hence, the perceived recontracting cost, in terms of conflict with existing employees, may be too high for employers to consider the alternative of paying the lower wage. Hence, the existing situation may fall within the inert areas of farm owners despite the existence of unemployed labor. We shall examine this question of the effect of unemployed labor on existing wage rates in greater detail in the next chapter.

For simplicity we have assumed throughout our discussion that wage rate will be equal to the marginal product of labor. However, this is not a necessary assumption in order to obtain our results—or to obtain reasonable results. Instead we can start with the assumption that the wage and value of the marginal product are unequal, but that the wage rises as the marginal product rises and vice versa. Furthermore, we assume that marginal product is positive when the wage is positive. Under these circumstances the results would be similar as labor migrates to the urban sector and more effort is put forth in the agricultural sector, wage rate rises although there is no presumption that one is equal to the other.

One of the awkward issues from a neoclassical viewpoint is the fact that even if the wage is equal to the value of the marginal productivity of labor, the individual who receives the wage is not necessarily going to keep it all. Part of it will be shared with members of his family on the basis of noneconomic considerations. Hence, it becomes too awkward to apply the usual utility analysis—this should involve an intra-familial utility analysis based on the division of consumption goods. In any event one can readily see that if we take this assumption into account, even in case of the family farm, it is quite possible for the utility of the marginal product received by the individual to be different from the utility of the marginal product which the individual's effort produces. Thus in the case of consumption sharing, if we consider only the utility of goods consumed by the individual worker, there is no reason to equate the marginal utility of the implicit wage with that of the product of effort.

CONSIDERATIONS AND CONCLUSIONS

The upshots of the analysis presented in this chapter are briefly as follows:

1. It is possible to have surplus labor and the simultaneous existence of a positive wage rate in the agricultural sector. Furthermore, surplus labor can exist even if the marginal product of labor is positive, provided this is interpreted in terms of a given effort level. But effort is a variable and its average level may change as a consequence of some of the labor migrating to the urban sector.

2. We end up with two concepts of surplus labor under conditions of disguised unemployment. In both cases there is in a sense an underutilization of the capacity of labor, although there is a full utilization of manpower. However, one has to distinguish the case in which there is simply incomplete utilization of effort and for which more effort would be forthcoming if less labor existed, as against the case of underutilization of effort without it necessarily increasing as labor is withdrawn. The existence of potentially additional effort versus actually obtaining additional effort out of this potential are two completely different matters.

3. Whether or not additional effort is put forth as a consequence of the removal of some manpower from the agricultural sector will depend on the distribution by farms of those that leave and the incentives created by the removal of manpower from specific farms. Such questions cannot be answered on an a priori basis, but they are critical questions in determining what happens when manpower is removed from the land.

On the whole the issue of surplus labor turns out to be somewhat more complicated once we allow for variable effort in the sense in which we have defined effort. We see that it is one thing to have potentially more effort and something else to have circumstances be such that more effort is in fact put forth upon the removal of a portion of the labor force. Nevertheless, in systems of effort sharing by workers, we can readily visualize circumstances under which some labor removals will result in some increases of the effort level. We have also seen that in principle there is nothing inconsistent between surplus labor and the existence of a positive wage rate in the agricultural sector, once we recognize effort as a variable.

5 | Migration and Urban Unemployment

MIGRATION AND ECONOMIC MOTIVATION

The economic theory of migration is not an especially well developed part of applied economics. While a great deal is known about migration patterns, the application of conventional microtheory to migration does not seem to predict what in fact occurs. If individuals were completely responsive to differentials in economic payoffs then we would expect that migration would eliminate wage differentials for labor of equal skills. If this were true on an international level then the problem of economic development as we know it would not exist. This is not to say that per capita income differences would disappear entirely, but that the difference in incomes that we know today would certainly be considerably less. In fact, the differences would be explained, for the most part, by the different skill mixes of those residing in different areas.

Some have argued that microtheory explains migration, since in econometric studies one usually finds that on the average signs of coefficients of a regression equation turn out to be in accordance with the theory.[1] However, such exercises, even if

---

[1] See A. K. Sen, *Employment, Technology, and Development* (Oxford: Clarendon Press, 1975), pp. 51–59, for a list of wage gap models.

they work out as expected, do not really test the theory but only one small aspect of it. It is certainly likely that areas in which the wage differentials are larger should have on the average more net in-migration than those in which the differentials are smaller. Nevertheless, this would be true even if the amounts of migration were minute as to have almost no influence on differentials themselves. In other words, it is quite possible that *of those who migrated,* more are attracted to areas where wage differentials are higher than to those where they are lower. But this would also be consistent with the theories which will not assume income maximization on the part of potential migrants. The fact that income differentials persist would suggest a high degree of inertia in the system and in fact responsiveness to differential opportunities may be very low.

One could argue that individuals cannot respond to differential economic opportunities across borders because of politically determined barriers to migration. While it would be interesting to determine to what extent such barriers explain income differentials, it seems clear that within countries where such barriers do not exist, large income differentials nevertheless persist.

The evidence collected and presented by Paul Bairoch[2] suggests that actual gaps within developing countries are today larger than they were in the current developed countries of the nineteenth century. In other words, the forces against a high degree of responsiveness seem on the average to be less today than they were in the past. Of course, this does not mean that migration responsiveness is less but mainly that the responsiveness of the more developed sectors to economic changes is less. However in some sense this suggests that migration is not sufficiently

[2] Paul Bairoch, *Urban Unemployment in Developing Countries* (Geneva: International Labor Office, 1973). Bairoch spends much time empirically viewing the extent of urban unemployment. In terms of migration on the theoretical level, he views income gap as the key cause of migration. Specifically, he isolates wages, incomes, and GNP/member of active population. He contrasts this to developed countries (U.S.A. in the nineteenth century) and says the gaps are wider today in LDC's. He also views the rise in education as a reason for migration.

responsive because of gaps involved. It would appear difficult to argue on the evidence that individuals are income maximizers in countries where migration is possible and yet income differentials continue. For example the differentials between São Paolo and northeast Brazil would argue against a theory of income maximization on the part of migrants.

An application of the X-efficiency theory readily fits some of the broad empirical results and known patterns in developing countries. If we assume that individuals operate in accordance with the theory of selective rationality, and that they do not respond to all economic opportunities, then the existence of dualism becomes much easier to understand. In a two-sector economy we would expect dualism to disappear if individuals did respond to superior opportunities in the higher per capita income sector, but if such responses are imperfect then the continuation of dualism is straight forward. In addition if we add the concept of inert areas, and visualize many potential migrants as individuals who have found occupations which are currently within their inert areas, it becomes easy to see rates of migration which would be much lower than that required to close the income gaps between different sectors.

A possible useful approach to migration theory is to visualize it as a potential innovative process. The superior economic opportunity in the other sectors represents an innovation which an individual could adopt, as it were, by moving to the other sector. We can utilize the X-efficiency theory of innovation to analyze this process. We assume that individuals are in their inert areas and that these have upper and lower bounds. With the aid of figure 5.1, we illustrate the process of migration. The line $\overline{M}$ represents the upper income bounds of the potential migrant's inert areas from the most sensitive towards the new opportunity to the least sensitive. Curve Ay represents the anticipated income from migrating. Similarly, line $\underline{M}$ represents the lower income bounds of those who are potential migrants. It is clearly possible for the curve Ay to be shaped in such a way that it cuts the $\overline{M}$ from above at some point so that the migration process is aborted long before there is enough migration to equalize returns to work between the two sectors. Average income in the agricultural sector is represented by the curve labelled y.

As the curves are drawn on figure 5.1 we see the actual amount of migration will be OA. The amount of migration necessary to achieve equality in wages between the sectors would be OB. If we considered a point beyond OA—let us say C, this would indicate that the wage necessary to induce migration is considerably above the actual wage in the agricultural sector, but it is still within the inert area so that migration does not take place. This is not to argue that this highly simplified picture of the situa-

Figure 5.1

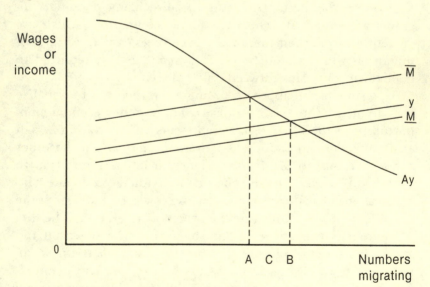

$\overline{M}$ = Upper-income bound of potential migrants
y = Average income in agricultural sector
Ay = Anticipated income in urban sector
$\underline{M}$ = Lower-income bound of potential migrants

tion corresponds to reality, but it illustrates how the inert area idea can explain the differences between the impact of the actual amount of migration as against the amount required to close the intersectoral wage gap.

Some of the reasons for an "inadequate" rate of migration to achieve equality of returns between sectors fall into the following categories:

1. *Peer group pressures.* Probably the main reason is the desire of individuals to remain with one's peers, which includes the nuclear family or the extended family. This would include other elements and motivations which involve group membership. Whether or not we interpret such motivations as economic is almost a matter of taste. If we assume utility maximization and we do not specify what it is that is to be maximized then the desire to be with kith and kin may be one of the elements maximized. In this sense it fits an economic interpretation. Nevertheless it is an element that goes counter to maximization of *income* by decision making units.

2. *Knowledge of alternative opportunities.* The extent to which different individuals will have knowledge of superior opportunities elsewhere will differ markedly between individuals. Two elements are intertwined in the question of available knowledge. One is access to knowledge and the other is the use of such access. An individual may have access to knowledge of superior opportunities and for a variety of reasons may not be motivated to obtain the necessary information. Where the latter is the case, this fits our overall concept of X-inefficiency due to motivational factors. It would seem likely that for a great many individuals in the lower income sector, a lack of knowledge may be attributed to the lack of motivation to obtain the necessary information.

We have argued in an earlier chapter that an important part of X-inefficiency is a lack of interest or willingness to take advantage of *all* the opportunities for economic improvement that may arise.

3. *Relative versus Absolute Incomes.* In previous discussions

we assume that whatever it is that is maximized it is the *absolute* magnitude independent of the achievement of others. However, recent evidence suggests that for many individuals relative position is a significant motivation. Hence, many individuals in the low income sector may not be induced to migrate because their relative income is high although their absolute income is low. To the extent that relative income dominates their considerations, they may choose to stay in the low income sector despite the fact that in terms of absolute income there is a significant advantage to migrating. In part this depends upon whether an individual prefers to be a "big fish" in a small pond versus a "small fish" in a large pond. The large pond may involve a higher absolute income, but the relative income may be lower and less inducive to the happiness of the individual.

Unquestionably, readers can think of many other reasons for an inadequate rate of migration to achieve equality of returns. The critical question is whether these additional reasons are to be classified in terms of standard economic motivations, in which in some sense individuals attempt to maximize income, and under which each decision making unit decides independently of others, or as against those reasons that come under the rubric of noneconomic motivations and nonindependent decision making. Among the latter we would include the concepts of inertia or being in an inert area.

An interesting aspect of migration literature is the recent emphasis on rural-urban migration, and the view that there has been, by and large, excess migration to urban areas. Part of the evidence of this is the large amount of actual or disguised unemployment in the urban areas of LDCs. Thus it would seem that on one hand we have less than adequate migration to equalize the rate of return, and on the other hand too much migration in terms of the ability of the urban sector to absorb migrants from rural areas. Part of the problem of simultaneously seeing too little and too much migration may be resolved by thinking of the deficit as a long range problem and of the excess as a short range one. Whether this is a correct resolution of the difference remains to be seen. My own view is that in general there is a deficit of migration, in that the excess is accounted for by a lack of flexibility in the urban economy. In any event we have argued that standard economic theory cannot explain either the deficit in the migration that exists or the short run surplus that appears to be evident in many developing countries.

It is probably correct to view the surplus aspect as part of a short run problem. If there were not a steady flow of migration but a fixed initial short run surplus, it seems likely that in the course of time the urban economy would absorb the temporary surplus. Why the surplus occurs has been analyzed in recent years in terms of the probability of obtaining a higher income in the urban area compared to the rural areas. There are two views of this probability calculus. One is the viewpoint brought forth by Todaro[3] which argues in terms of the *mathematical value* of the probability of obtaining a job in the urban area as compared to the *certain* income in the agricultural sector. Thus if there is a ninety percent chance of obtaining a job in the urban area then one multiplies the urban income by .9 and compares it to the value of the rural income. A somewhat more sophisticated measure has been proposed by Sen[4] in which the comparison is made of the utility of a certain income in the rural area versus the utility of the income of a probable job in the urban area. We will want to argue that either way of looking at the problem ignores a good deal of migration which takes place for noneconomic reasons, or which takes place out of inertia as a consequence of individuals not returning to the countryside after a tentative attempt to "make it" in the city, despite the fact that the rural income may be higher than its urban counterpart.

[3] M. P. Todaro, "A Model of Labor Migration and Urban Unemployment In Lesser Developed Countries," *American Economic Review* (1969).
[4] See A. K. Sen, "Peasants and Dualism with or without Surplus Labor," *Journal of Political Economy* 74 (1966).

THE EMPLOYMENT ABSORPTION PROBLEM

Consider briefly two conventional approaches to the urban employment absorption problem: (1) the neoclassical approach which would result if institutional wage rigidities and other market imperfections were eliminated and (2) an "engineering approach" which visualizes a rigid technology and a fixed capital-employment ratio.

The neoclassical economists' approach assumes that there is a high degree of substitutability between inputs. If markets work and an excess labor supply exists at the outset, wages fall (relative to capital costs), and as wages fall there is an inducement for labor to be substituted for capital so that eventually all labor is employed. If the existing stock of capital limits the substitutability of labor for other inputs, it is presumed that low wage rates will encourage the introduction of more labor intensive capital so that an increased demand for labor results. According to this view it is primarily necessary to eliminate institutional or political rigidities in the labor market so that wages are sufficiently flexible to operate as equilibrating variables. Lower wages also decrease the supply since they decrease the wage differential between urban wages and other wages, and hence decrease the flow of labor to urban areas.

Now, there are indeed institutional and political rigidities in many labor markets. However, we shall argue below that their removal would not necessarily be sufficient to yield an urban full employment equilibrium.

What might be viewed as a simplistic engineering approach visualizes very limited technological choice and very little substitution of labor for other inputs, and hence a fairly fixed capital-employment ratio in each industry. If this view were correct, urban labor demand would be a simple function of the rate of urban capital accumulation. The distribution of the demand for capital to different industries would be determined by income elasticities of demand for the products produced by the capital. Whether or not full employment would result would depend entirely on whether the rate of urban capital accumulation was sufficiently high. The evidence suggests that technology is very far from rigid and that the assumptions behind this view are incorrect. Nevertheless, we will want to argue that inadequate capital accumulation may result in unemployment, but for entirely different reasons than those that depend on technological rigidities.

A SIMPLE URBAN LABOR MARKET MODEL

We now sketch a simple model of the labor market. Supply is assumed to be significantly influenced by net internal migration to the urban area. The demand for labor is determined by the wage rate and some related variables. The wage rate itself will be determined by special considerations analyzed in the next section. The model is limited to a single *period*.

The basic variables are as follows:

M, the amount of *net* internal migration *to* urban area within the working age groups.

W, the average urban wage rate.

E, the *percent* of the urban labor force that is employed.

e, the *amount* of employment in the urban area. This is essentially the number of jobs available.

W_a, the wage rate in agriculture, or "elsewhere."

L, the labor force at the beginning of the period.

L_e, urban population not previously in the labor force that enters the labor force.

R, labor that retires at the beginning of the period.

S, the supply of labor in the urban area—a flow.

The basic net migration relationship is:

(0) $w_a = given$

(1a) $M = f_m (W, E)$

Migration depends on the wage rate and on the percent of the labor force employed. It is assumed that the non-urban wage W_a is given. W_a is basically the opportunity cost of labor from elsewhere. The larger the urban wage compared to the non-urban wage, the larger the amount of net migration. Beyond some point migration varies inversely with the employment rate. That is, the greater the level of unemployment, the lower the net migration rate.[5]

Labor supply depends on the labor force L at the beginning of the period, the urban labor that enters at various age groups L_e, the labor that retires R, and net migration M. Thus, we have a supply of labor S for the period.

(1b) $S = L + L_e - R + M$

For simplicity we can assume that retirements are entirely functions of the age structure at the beginning of the period. In this formulation, since the age structure during the previous period is assumed to be known, then the number of people who retire is also known. Hence, retirements are given. Of those *not* in the labor force in the previous period, some are potential entrants which depend only in part on the given age structure. That is, age structure will determine in part those who are in school, who leave school, women who marry and leave the labor force, etc. However, in part we may assume that entry into the labor force depends on the wage rate and the employment rate. In sum, entry to the labor force depends on the same variables as net migration. We write the equation as follows:

(1c) $L_e + M = f_u (W,E)$

[5] This relation can be viewed as a very simple version of the Todaro model of net migration previously cited.

For every value of L_e and M the supply of labor S is determined since L and R are both based on parameters given at the beginning of the period. In a more sophisticated model we could assume that retirements depend also on the wage rate, the employment rate, and other variables. But for our purposes we want to keep everything down to essentials. Hence we can write the basic equation which determines the supply of labor as follows:

$$(1) \qquad\qquad S = f_s\,(W,E)$$

To simplify matters we assume that aggregate urban employment as a *stock* depends only on the urban wage rate, given W_a. Hence, we have:

$$(2) \qquad\qquad e = f_e(W)$$

The employment *rate* is defined as the following:

$$(3) \qquad\qquad E = \frac{e}{S}$$

The relation between labor supply, wages and the employment rate is summarized in figure 5.2. The line marked $\overline{W}\,\overline{E}$ in quadrant I indicates the set of *equilibrium* wage-employment rates. The idea behind $\overline{W}\,\overline{E}$ is as follows: from equation (2) for each wage on the ordinate there is a level of employment $\underline{e}$; and for each level of E on the abscissa there is a wage W so that its associated value of S from equation (1) (and level of $\underline{e}$) yields the employment rate E. We see that we could conceive of an equilibrium set of labor supply-employment rate levels for every wage level. The related labor-supply rates are illustrated in quadrant two of figure 5.2. Given the labor supply function (equation [1]), $\overline{W}\,\overline{E}$ is the only set of values that can result.

Quadrants one and two in figure 5.2 show the values of S and W and E when they are consistent with each other in accord-

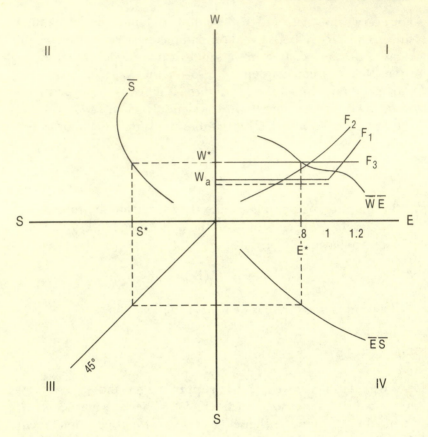

Figure 5.2

ance with equations (1), (2), and (3). To obtain a solution we have to introduce a relationship that will determine the actual wage. This involves a "wage-offer function," one example of which is the curve F_2 in figure 5.2. It completes the system.

Formally we have here a five equation system in five variables, W_a, W, S, E, and e. However, W_a is given and E, determined in equation (3), is simply a definition. Therefore, basically we have three variables W, e, and S, and so far two behavioral equations:

the labor supply equation (1) and the employment creation equation (2). To complete the system we need a wage offer function.

$$(4) \qquad\qquad W = F_i \, (?)$$

Equation (4) indicates the puzzle we face, solutions for which are suggested in the next section. We consider alternative wage offer functions and possible reasons for them. However, we shall see that not all wage offer functions are consistent with an equilibrium of less than full employment.

As illustrated in figure 5.2, the intersection of F_2 (one of the candidates for a wage offer function) and the wage-employment locus $\overline{W}\,\overline{E}$ determine the exact wage rate W^*, the related equilibrium rate E^*, and the related equilibrium labor supply rate S^*.

But the significant question for our purposes remains the *nature* of the wage-offer function. We consider below three possible alternatives marked F_1, F_2, and F_3 in figure 5.2.

ALTERNATIVE WAGE-OFFER FUNCTIONS

The Neoclassical Wage-Offer Function

According to neoclassical theory the wage rate fluctuates to clear the labor market. To simplify matters we assume that *some* laborers could always return to the area from which they came and receive the "elsewhere" wage W_a. Hence W_a is paid if there is unemployment, or W is greater than W_a if there is excess demand for labor. If there is a temporary excess supply of labor and W is greater than W_a, then W falls until the excess supply is eliminated. Thus the neoclassical wage-offer function is at the level W_a until the full employment point, and then rises towards a higher level. This is illustrated by F_1 in quadrant one. However, experience suggests that we frequently observe the coexistence of considerable urban unemployment and an urban wage level (W) above the agricultural level (W_a). Hence, we must consider other possible wage-offer functions.

The "Efficiency Wage" Hypothesis

Another possibility is that firms pay a wage above the transfer wage W_a despite the existence of unemployment and despite any apparent necessity to do so in order to attract labor. Such behavior is by no means irrational. We have to separate (1) the price to attract labor and (2) the price to attract *effort*. We assume that any wage greater than W_a will attract some labor from "elsewhere" if E is sufficiently large. Now, it would be rational to pay a higher wage than W_a if this would result in a more than proportional increase in efficiency per man and resultant value of output. A basic point to be kept in mind is that (1) *the effort level* and (2) *the quality of effort* are usually undetermined or only partially or vaguely determined by the employment contract. Paying a higher wage than "necessary" may involve a tacit agreement between the employer and the employees that he expects a proportionately greater quantitative and/or qualitative effort level for the higher wage. We need not concern ourselves with the exact details of how such tacit or partially tacit agreements are worked out.[6] They may come about through employer selection of employees who are responsive to such inducements, or through norms of work established in the firm which indirectly support such patterns and so on.

The employment relation is rarely unconstrained. The constraints frequently include (1) seniority rules, (2) agreements

---

[6] For a brief survey of empirical evidence in favor of this possibility, see Robert L. Opsahl and Marvin D. Dunnette, "The Role of Financial Compensation in Industrial Motivation," *Management and Motivation,* eds. Victor H. Vroom and Edward L. Deci, Penguin Modern Management Readings (New York: Penguin Books, 1972). The main reference to a study in an underdeveloped country is the one by H. C. Ganuli, "An Inquiry into Incentives for Working in an Engineering Factory," *The Industrial Journal of Social Work* 15, pp. 30–40.

and customs against firing employees once employed, (2) semi-property rights in a job, and so on. The employer may sensibly feel that once stuck with certain employees, he might as well treat them well and obtain, in return, a high level of effort. On the other hand, employees have weapons against demands for effort without compensating inducements. In addition to the almost ubiquitous existence of an anti-"rate busting" morality enforced by peer group pressures, there are in some cases negotiated trade union rules vis-à-vis some aspects of effort, as well as slowdowns, strikes, and industrial sabotage where workers wish to show their displeasure with existing arrangements. The main point to be kept in mind is that where the dimensions of effort (e.g., choice of activities, quality of activities, pace of effort, and time worked) are variables which are not rigidly determined in advance in the employment contract,[7] it is quite possible that higher wages, up to a point, may be associated with more than proportionate increases in productivity.

The nature of the basic relationship involved is illustrated in figure 5.3. In the figure, W is the wage rate and the abscissa $\frac{Q}{L}$ is output per man. Rays drawn from the origin represent a constant wage per unit of output. (If the ordinate is effort, then each ray represents a constant wage cost per unit of effort.) Obviously the cost minimizing employer would wish to minimize the wage cost per unit of effort (or per unit of output). A series of "effort-employment-rate" curves marked ϵE_1, ϵE_2, ϵE_3, etc., represents the appropriate wage-effort relationships based on different values of E. The assumption here is that the lower the employment rate, the higher the effort that will be put forth, up to a point, other things equal. The shape of the wage-efficiency relation ϵE_1 or ϵE_2, etc., indicates that up to some point

---

[7] On this point see Harvey Leibenstein, "Organization or Frictional Equilibria, X-Efficiency, and the Rate of Innovation," *Quarterly Journal of Economics,* November 1969. See also, Harvey Leibenstein, "X-Efficiency and Competition," *Journal of Political Economy,* June 1973.

the higher the wage the greater the effort (or the output), but that beyond some point the effort effect of a higher wage disappears and the curves become vertical. Points of tangency between the wage-effort functions and rays from the origin are minimum cost points per unit of effort and hence they represent the locus (1ϵ in figure 5.3) of efficient wage effort relations. Thus, we can read from figure 5.3 a set of points (on 1ϵ) such that each point represents a wage rate and a related employment rate which minimizes the wage cost per unit of effort. This set of points is shown in figure 5.2 by the curve F_2.

Figure 5.3

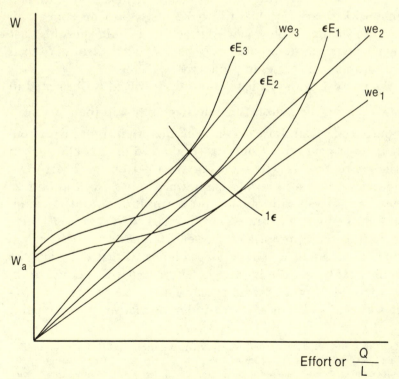

$E_3 > E_2 > E_1$

$w_{e3} > w_{e2} > w_{e1}$

The shape of the curve F_2 is based on the notion that the lower the employment rate, the greater the extent that people want to hold on to jobs, and the greater the tacit effort level, and hence the *optimal* efficiency wage rises as the employment level rises. However, there is no reason why the function F_2 could not intersect the equilibrium $\overline{W}\,\overline{E}$ curve at less than full employment as illustrated in quadrant one of figure 5.2.

The X-Efficiency Ratchet

A third possibility is that the wage rate is determined by historical conditions in the industry and cannot be changed by deviations in the demand or the supply of labor unless the excess demand or excess supply become exceptionally large. Consider the case of a well established firm that pays a wage W greater than W_a. While unemployed labor is willing to accept jobs at less than the going wage rate the firm may find it difficult or impossible to enter into such contracts. We limit ourselves first to the case in which all workers are paid the same wage. If additional workers are hired at a lower wage then the firm has to recontract with its old labor force for a lower wage. But the old labor force is not without power to prevent such recontracting. Apart from the possibility of a formalized strike, it can slow down the pace of its effort as well as the quality of its work in various ways. In other words the existing work force can exact a psychological and economic cost if the employer tries to recontract the wage rate. The rational employer would take this cost into account and would not attempt such recontracting if the disutility of the cost is greater than the utility of the gain. This is the essence of the theory of inert areas (and X-inefficiency) in which economic agents do not move to what appear to be superior positions because the utility cost of such movements are greater than the utility gain.[8]

New firms are likely to be in a similar position. Although

[8] See Harvey Leibenstein, "Organizational or Frictional Equilibria, X-Efficiency, and the Rate of Innovation," *Quarterly Journal of Economics,* November 1969.

they do not have to recontract with an existing labor force, if they pay their labor a lower wage than that paid by competing firms then labor is likely to feel resentful and reduce its effort level accordingly. To some degree the same is likely to be true if firms attempt to discriminate in wages between those newly hired and those who have been in their employ before. Thus, we may visualize an X-efficiency wage ratchet at the going-wage level, say W^*, despite the fact that there is an excess supply of labor on the market. In figure 5.2 this is shown by the curve F_3.

EFFORT AND CHOICE OF TECHNIQUE

What kind of capital should firms choose in the face of unemployment? The traditional view is that unemployment in flexible labor markets leads to lower wages, which in turn lead to the adoption of labor saving technologies.[9] But this argument fails to distinguish between (1) the market for and buying of labor time and (2) the provision of labor *effort*. We therefore consider possibilities under which this distinction is maintained in order to see if it can provide an explanation for the observation and frequent assertion that capital equipment installed in developing countries is inappropriate in view of the transfer wage (or the shadow price) of labor—i.e., the equipment chosen is more capital intensive than warranted.

Consider two possibilities: one in which the capital is "effort neutral," and the other in which the capital is "effort stretching." If capital has no effect on the provision of effort, then the capital introduced will be the one appropriate to $W^* > W_a$ in figure 5.2, assuming that the appropriate wage offer functions are either F_2 or F_3. In those two cases, since the equilibrium wage is above the transfer cost W_a, then the technique chosen

---

[9] We leave out of consideration the switching controversy possibilities. It seems unlikely to me that the conditions necessary for re-switching are empirically significant. The argument should not rest on such a slender reed. For a simple explanation of the switching problem see Joan Robinson, *The Accumulation of Capital* (Homewood, IL: Richard E. Irwin Co., 1956), pp. 109–110.

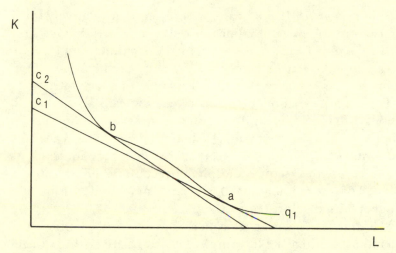

Figure 5.4

and capital introduced will be more capital intensive than would be the case if the wage function was the neoclassical one F_1.

An interesting possibility is one in which capital is "effort-stretching." This possibility is illustrated in figure 5.4 which employs the usual elementary choice of technique diagram. In figure 5.4, K are units of capital and L are units of labor. Normal isoquants are convex from the origin. However, one can visualize a *segment* of an isoquant that is concave. An interpretation of such a segment is as follows: There exists a set of techniques such that for given equal increases in capital the required amount of labor decreases to an increasing degree. This is the result not only of effort stretching per se, but of a sufficiently high degree of "effort stretching" to counteract the otherwise diminishing rate of substitution of capital for labor, as capital is increased.

In figure 5.4 we show both isoquant and isocost curves in which the isoquants have an *increasing* marginal rate of substitution *segment*. In that case, we can see that relatively small increases in the price of labor can result in a considerable shift in the degree of capital intensity of the technique and equipment adopted. This is shown by the shift of the isocost lines from c_1 to c_2 for a relatively small increase in the wage rate.

Thus, once we allow for effort stretching capital, we have a rationale for introducing fairly capital intensive techniques in relatively low wage countries. It should be emphasized that for the segment *ab* in figure 5.4, capital per man may increase. As we move up the isoquant, capital per unit of effort can decrease. For a given amount of labor the new capital stimulates a higher level of effort per worker.

It is difficult to derive set conclusions from all of these considerations. All that we have argued is that relatively high wages in urban areas, and relatively capital intensive techniques can be seen, once the effort offer is introduced as a consideration, as fairly rational responses to the existing situation. Unfortunately, such responses turn out to be consistent with the existence of actual or disguised unemployment.

It is possible that if the rate of capital accumulation is great enough, unemployment may gradually be eliminated despite the fact that the capital introduced is relatively labor saving. However, on purely a priori grounds nothing could be said about the relative magnitudes involved so as to determine whether high but not implausible rates of investment could lead to full employment under these circumstances.

One need not draw pessimistic conclusions from this analysis. It would seem reasonable to speculate that there are limits to the extent to which increases in capital per man can continue to be effort stretching. It would seem reasonable to suppose that in this analysis, as well as in others, we hit diminishing returns at some point. Another way of saying this is that it is unlikely that "mechanization" can induce significant increases in effort indefinitely. Therefore, we should expect that the concave section of the isoquants are indeed segments of rather limited length. Beyond some point the effort stretching advantage of mechanization should peter out and the normal relationships between wage rates, choice of technique, and employment absorption should once again become the significant ones. Also, the effort stretching effect is likely to be relatively more important in manufacturing. As a country develops there is a limit to the expansion of the manufacturing sector. More and more labor gradually moves into services where, compared to manufacturing, effort stretching mechanization is, on the average, likely to be less significant.

6 | Savings, Investment, and Development

There is a qualitative sense that distinguishes the growth problems of a developing economy from that of a developed economy. This sense can only be incompletely perceived on the basis of traditional economic analysis. To see what is involved consider the diagramatic visualization of the problem. In figure 6.1 we show a curve marked *PGP* which indicates the potential growth path of an idealized country that passes from an underdeveloped stage to a developed stage. The S-shaped curve has three phases in it marked by a slow growth stage, a very rapid growth phase, and again a slow growth stage. The initial phase represents the close to zero growth of an underdeveloped economy. The final stage represents the relatively slow growth of a mature economy. The phase in between represents the extremely rapid growth of an idealized developing economy which passed in some optimal fashion from the underdeveloped to the developed stage.

The object of this chapter is to discuss possible elements suggested by general X-efficiency theory which may help to explain why growth rates differ in different countries and why growth rates differ in the same country at different periods. We shall be

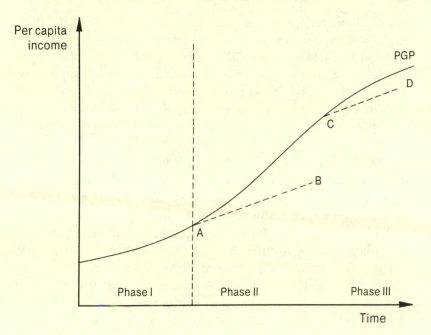

Figure 6.1

particularly concerned with the problem of why some growth
rates are very low compared to their potential—i.e., why actual
growth rates may be very much lower than they could be given
the nature of the country, the *stage* of its development, and both
its actual or potential human and nonhuman resources. In particular, we shall focus attention on various aspects of the capital
absorption problem as it frequently manifests itself in developing countries.

Stage theories of development have not fared especially well,
and it is probably best not to take such theories very seriously.
One possible reason for this is that the process of development
as it actually takes place does not suggest a uniform enough pattern, nor is it sufficiently uniform in its components, to fit what
we observe in different countries into different stages. Neverthe-

less (without taking the matter too seriously), there exist different *potentials* for growth under different circumstances so that such *gross* differences should be distinguished. We shall focus on the distinction between the cases in which a developing country can borrow and benefit from the techniques of production available in advanced countries, as against those cases in which the opportunities for borrowing are either limited or do not exist at all.

The basic idea is illustrated in table 6.1. The two possibilities shown vertically are (1) the case in which the developing country can borrow a great many new techniques or new products from the developed countries and (2) the situations in which no such borrowing is possible or the amount of borrowing that can take place is fairly unimportant. Across we show the two possibilities under which the country cannot take advantage of the techniques available elsewhere as against the case of the country that can take advantage of opportunities that come from outside the economy. This results in four possibilities only three of which are significant. These are shown clockwise in table 6.1 as phases one, two, and three. It must be quite evident that phase two allows for greater possibilities of growth than phase one. It will be this phase that will be emphasized in our discussion. We shall be especially concerned with the problem as to why some countries have low rates of growth in phase two despite

Table 6.1

	No capacity to use new technology	Can use new technology
Technological borrowing possible	I	II
No technological borrowing possible		III

the fact that this represents a high growth potential phase for the country involved.

Let us now look at the three stages in sequence more carefully to see if there is any inherent logic in these stages. The underdeveloped stage represents the very slow growth of an economy which is relatively isolated from the economic process of modernization. Such an economy is essentially closed to the ideas and techniques of the advanced economies. Thus it uses what are sometimes referred to as primitive techniques of production and operates in terms of a zero or low levels of growth which reflect traditional techniques of production well known to that particular economy. Some variants of a classical or Malthusian model can help to explain the workings of this particular economy. Its rates of investment are relatively low but are sufficient to provide for a widening of the capital stock so as to absorb the labor force growth determined by the rate of population growth consistent with the fertility rates endogenous to such an economy. For ease of exposition let us use the conventional Harrod-Domar categories and think of the investment-capital output ratio relationships. Suppose the capital-output ratio is three to one—that is, it takes three additional units of capital of the type that exists in the economy to produce one additional unit of output, if there is adequate additional labor to man the additional capital. Now suppose that the investment rate is 9% and the population growth rate as well as the labor force growth rate is 3%. This should lead to an increase in output of 3% which allows the expansion of the labor force to produce at the same rate as the existing labor force. If there were less than a 3% increase in labor force, then there would be a scarcity of labor, while the more than 3% growth rate would lead to visible or disguised unemployment. Such an economy would be growing at a zero rate. We can also allow for the gradual improvement of techniques based on the knowledge and the growth of productive knowledge internal to such an economy which would lead to a very slight growth rate.

Of course, an economy which would be in phase one would not necessarily grow smoothly within that phase. There may be periods of relatively poor harvests and inefficient urban production so that we may have negative per capita income growth followed by relatively good harvests and catching up on urban efficiency and positive growth rates. Nevertheless we can visualize a variety of such fluctuations bounded by a floor and a ceiling consistent with the low per capita income growth rates associated with phase one.

We can develop a somewhat similar model for the third phase. The structure of such an economy would be relatively different, and its growth potential would depend on somewhat different factors. To be brief, such an economy would be mostly urban, and its growth would depend primarily on the increased manufacture of goods in urban areas. The net growth rate of its population would be extremely low and perhaps in an idealized state it would be zero. Hence, all of its growth would increase per capita output rather than some of it being required for the absorption of a growing labor force. Finally, its growth would be determined entirely by the *invention* of improved techniques of production, of physical goods, and of services. Since the rate of inventiveness is limited and fairly low, we would expect such an economy to grow at a low rate, somewhere between 0.5% to 2% per year. Although the structural elements of the economies in both phase one and phase three are different, they are similar in that their equilibrium growth rates are rather low, and, to the extent that growth occurs, it depends on endogenously determined improvement of productive technique, which is limited in its capacity to increase the productive power of the economy. The growth rates in the two cases may be different from each other but their order of magnitude is very different from that of the developing economy.

The developing economy in phase two proceeds along what may be called the "grand traverse." It faces very different possibilities of improvement than the phase three economy or than the phase one economy faced. We shall see that it also faces additional pitfalls. To indicate what is involved let us visualize the situation in the following artificial way. Suppose that there exists a book of blueprints describing all the existing techniques of production available. Suddenly a new book is discovered which includes the existing techniques but also includes additional techniques which increase output manyfold compared to the existing techniques. How would the economy react to such a discovery?

However the economy would react to such a discovery, it is clear that new possibilities for growth are involved. The possibility of moving from the techniques in book one to the superior techniques in blueprint book two allows for considerable expansion of output that was not available before. The economy is now faced with the problem of adopting and adapting the new techniques of production that it copies from the new book without the economy evolving naturally, as it would if only the old book of techniques had been available. Finally, the savings rate which was quite adequate for maintaining equilibrium growth now turns out to be a bottleneck.

It is of special interest to see that during the great traverse phase the limiting factors change. In phase one the limiting factor is the knowledge of new techniques. In this idealized model, it would not do very much good to have had a higher rate of savings since it could not be absorbed. At this point, limited knowledge would not make it possible to carry out the capital deepening to any greater degree. However with the new techniques available there are now a great many opportunities to improve output through increased investment. In phase one investment goods were used in part to replace existing capital goods as they wore out and in part to provide outfits of capital for the growing labor force. But now replacement is no longer a sufficient demand creating factor for capital goods. Even if new capital is introduced at the going replacement rate, it would still result in an increased growth rate since the book two level of techniques allows for the introduction of more efficient machinery than the machinery worn-out. However the new machinery, designed on the basis of book two, is now so efficient that it pays to replace the old machinery long before it wears out according to the previous rate of obsolescence. Clearly the old rate of savings is no longer sufficient to take advantage of all the opportunities for investment in the system.

Three basic problems face the economy in phase two: (1) how to choose among the variety of new techniques available those most suitable to it, (2) how to adapt some of these new techniques to a basically underdeveloped labor force which is different from the labor force on the basis of which the new techniques have been created in the developed countries, and (3) how to increase the savings rate to take advantage of the new opportunities for investment. In some idealized sense there may be an optimal way in which all of these problems can be solved. At the optimal rate, the underdeveloped economy represents the rate at which, at its most optimistic, it can grow to the phase of the developed economy. The optimal rate is illustrated by the steep incline of the curve in figure 6.1. In actuality neither developed nor developing countries will be growing at their optimal rate. Nevertheless there will be a difference in the nature of the growth pattern. This is illustrated by the curve marked CD for the developed country growth pattern and AB for the underdeveloped. Even though AB is not optimal, it contains the possibility of a more rapid growth rate than under CD. Furthermore AB is characterized by the introduction of new capital which contains mostly the borrowing of techniques not indigenous to the country. The developed countries introduce capital which depends largely on the invention of techniques in their own economy or in similarly developed economies.

SAVINGS, INVESTMENT ABSORPTION, AND X-INEFFICIENCY

Once we have the image of the grand traverse of development, we have an idea of the outer bound growth rates open to a de-

veloping economy. From the actual experience of some rapidly
growing economies in the post World War II era, we also have
an idea of the orders of magnitude involved. There have been
a number of economies, of which Japan is an example, which
have grown from 7% to 10% for over a decade. While such
rates cannot be sustained indefinitely, these rates are over five-
fold the rate that we might expect an economy to grow without
borrowing any superior techniques in any sense. Thus, we can
readily say that there is an order of magnitude difference between the optimally growing rate and the nondevelopment rate.
Nevertheless we would be foolish to expect that once an economy enters the phase of technique borrowing, that it would
necessarily expect to grow at a rate approximating the grand
traverse rate.

We have already suggested in the previous section one of the
obstacles that may arise in achieving smooth transition from
phase one to phase two. Mainly the savings rate appropriate for
phase one growth is unlikely to be appropriate for phase two
growth. Hence, to the extent that there are inertial elements in
changing the savings rate this may set a limit to increasing the
investment rate. We may separate the savings rate into two components, savings by households and savings by firms. Household
savings should depend, in part, on conventional patterns of
consumption. Part of the inert areas operative in any economy
is likely to control the consumption levels of households. This
may be especially true in developing economies where the level
of consumption is sufficiently low so that there is pressure to
increase consumption to a greater extent than increases in income. We may consider the case of that portion of households
whose income is temporarily low enough so that their consumption level is above their income level and all that is achieved
for a rise in the income level is to enable such households to re-
pay debts. Nevertheless the previous debt determined consumption level is lower than its customary level, and, as a result,
when incomes rise the consumption level rises at least propor-

tionately. Thus inertial elements create considerable inelasticity in expanding the saving rates of households.

A somewhat similar argument to the above can be developed for savings which come out of firms. Such savings arise through the process of ploughing back firm profits. But unless profits are very high, savings cannot increase. Hence, if profit levels remain approximately the same in the early parts of phase two as they were in phase one, then we can visualize a strong inertial system operating which would inhibit any rapid expansion of the profit rate. In a sense, we get into a vicious circle in this area. Profit rates which are anticipated must be sufficiently high and must occur sufficiently rapidly after investment, so that they lead to rapid rates of investment which in turn result in high profit rates. However, we shall see that it is precisely the connections between various points in this process which lead to the difficulties involved. In other words, anticipated high profits may not materialize because the investments do not lead to effective enough utilization of the possibilities inherent in the new production processes to produce sufficiently higher output levels, which in turn would produce sufficiently higher profits.

INVESTMENT ABSORPTION PROBLEMS

Another way of viewing the problem is to suggest that it is not helpful to produce higher savings rates if these savings rates cannot be invested effectively. Furthermore there is a connection between the creation of savings rates and their effective investment possibilities. The considerations involved have also been referred to as the problem of the absorption of investment. This really involves two interrelated questions. One depends on the supply of entrepreneurship, while the other depends on the extent to which potential investment can lead to the effective utilization of increased inputs. These aspects are related since if it is anticipated that the inputs cannot be utilized effectively, then there is unlikely to be any entrepreneurial supply which would create the demand for the investment goods. Hence there is a sense in which it all boils down to the degree of X-efficiency in production utilizing new and improved types of capital. We now turn to treat these elements separately, but we must keep in mind that these elements are closely connected despite the fact that we can only discuss them systematically by handling them one at a time.

In the postwar world one way of overcoming the savings bottleneck to growth has been a system of international grants and loans. While such loans have frequently been on too small a scale to make a significant impact, there are cases where it has been argued that the main problem has been that the receiving country has found it difficult to absorb the additional capital involved. There is a certain plausibility in such arguments, and we can see that such arguments can be developed and expanded on the basis of earlier ideas. Difficulty in absorbing additional capital may arise on the one hand because of insufficient entrepreneurial supply and on the other because of low levels of X-efficiency in production involving the new capital and new techniques.

Consider the case of entrepreneurial supply. We have suggested previously that entrepreneurship does not necessarily represent a universalized skill. Thus there may be people capable of entrepreneurial activities in agriculture but not in manufacturing, while some may have these capabilities in some types of manufacturing but not in others. To the extent that entrepreneurs have to be gap fillers and input completers, they may be able to do so in some areas of the economy but not in others. The entrepreneurial supply required to maintain phase one may be quite small and may require only traditional skills, in the sense that the entrepreneurs may be well practiced gap fillers and input completers in a traditional range of industries with well-known techniques of production. However to proceed from phase one to phase two would require a larger entrepreneurial supply involving gap filling and input completing activities for new techniques of production and to some extent for new products. Furthermore we have also argued that not all those who possess entrepreneurial skills will necessarily use them since their skills may be used either more effectively or may give their possessors greater satisfaction in other pursuits. In other words, the psychological rewards to entrepreneurship may not be enough to shift individuals away from their application of effort from nonentrepreneurial pursuits to entrepreneurship. Because new products and techniques are involved in phase two, there is likely to be a greater risk element involved in dealing with unfamiliar aspects of entrepreneurship.

The new type of productive activities pertinent to phase two are likely to involve different kinds of motivational environments and different structures than those which predominate in phase one. Such new structures may lead to a greater degree of X-inefficiency, or at least be prone to operating to a higher degree of X-inefficiency than in more conventional forms of organization. It may be useful to go through some of the possible differences involved and speculate on some of the likely outcomes. For instance the unit size of the new firms may have to be larger than the conventional ones. Furthermore since the conventional ones may be limited to family operated firms and the new ones may go beyond the family structure, new patterns of interpersonal interdependencies are involved and new types of emerging motivational forces are implied. Thus the effort positions that would normally be chosen by family members would not be the ones chosen by strangers. In addition the inert areas chosen by family members may be smaller than those that would be chosen by strangers. This implies that the principal-agent relationships between non-family members are likely to be quite different from those for family members. Finally the inherent motivational forces in terms of selective rationality may involve lower levels of rationality than would be the case for the complete family firm. The procedure we have followed in this paragraph has been to go through six of the basic components of general X-efficiency theory and to show how the results would differ between the family firm and the non-family firm. We also imply that in many contexts a plausible case could be made for the lower X-efficiency of the non-family firm versus the family firm.

The notion expressed in the previous paragraph would seem to argue against the fact that family firms have gradually disappeared as economic development has taken place. But for the most part this may be due to the size limitations inherent in the family firm and in the economies of scale which are not a function of size but which depend on the capacity to use more efficient capital when scales of operations are larger.

The main point of this analysis is that the economic conditions sufficient for the very limited growth that exists in phase one do not necessarily contain the seeds to allow for the absorption of investment that would lead to the very rapid rate of growth possible in phase two. We have seen that we can approach the analysis of this program from three viewpoints. The first is through the characteristics that determine the rate of supply of entrepreneurship; the second is through the various components that distinguish X-efficiency theory from neoclassical theory; and the third is through the application of some of these ideas to the problem of innovation.

Innovation can take place through two basic means: (1) the introduction of new firms using new techniques and (2) the introduction of these elements into existing firms. We have implicitly considered the new firm problem in discussing the limitations imposed by the low supply of entrepreneurship. In what follows let us limit our attention to the introduction of new techniques or new products by existing firms. While on the whole this problem is relatively complex and specific conditions in different industries will have an important influence on the outcome, there are certain general remarks that can be made. To start with we consider the introduction of a new technique and later consider the related problems of introducing new inputs, new consumer goods, new services, and so on.

Why should a firm selling a well-established product want to introduce a new technique? Under what it would consider normal conditions, it is likely to be quite happy with the existing technique. The more pleased it is with the existing technique, the wider would be its inert areas. To be more specific, the firm as such is neither pleased nor displeased with anything, and only members of the firm can have such feelings. But if things are going well with various members, then these members' effort positions are likely to be in inert areas with fairly wide bounds vis-à-vis new opportunities that exist outside the firm. But these opportunities are likely to be known only in a very vague sort of way. In order to take advantage of them there has to be clear cut effort put forth in completely new directions in order to discover the detailed nature of the new technique, as well as to determine all the changes that have to take place in order to introduce them successfully. By the very nature of things there must be a risk involved in shifting to a new technique which involves a new production experience as against using techniques whose details and pitfalls are well understood on the basis of past experience. Thus we see that unless there is considerable promise in the new technique, a great many sensible reasons would seem to exist for not shifting to the new technique. This would be true even if the firm was a monopolist in the product market. While on the one hand its market position would allow it to pass on potential losses to consumers if the new technique failed, on the other hand there is absolutely no pressure to adopt the new technique since there is no fear that a competing firm will get ahead of the monopolist by having the advantage of being an earlier adopter.

Now consider the competitive case. Do early adopters have a special advantage? From a neoclassical viewpoint under which firms are assumed to minimize cost, the early adopter would have a lower cost than its competitors and would be in a position to charge a somewhat lower market price and hence would be able to expand its market share at the expense of the market shares of the competitors. But if firms do not have any predetermined mechanical capacity to minimize costs then it no longer follows that the new technique will lead to *actual* lower costs. Of course, the new technique must contain the possibility of lower costs, otherwise it would presumably not be seriously entertained as an alternative to the existing mode of production. But the new elements in the new technique may result in higher actual X-inefficiency and hence actual higher costs. Thus existing firms may very well prefer to see other firms take on the experiment of trying out the new technique. Only after the experiment proves successful by other firms would it be necessary for the firms that wait to try it out. If it is unsuccessful elsewhere then the waiting firms have the advantage of not having experienced the losses of the experimenting firms.

But suppose that all firms think in the same manner as our waiting firms do. Will the innovation ever take place? If all firms see an advantage to waiting then, of course, the innovative process will never get started. Introducing the concept of inert areas for the significant decision makers in each firm responsible for introducing innovations, we would expect that the innovation would not be introduced unless the gain, directly or indirectly, to the decision maker goes beyond the inert area bounds. To the extent that feelings about the risks of being an initial innovator dampens the expected gain from innovation, the innovation will not get started unless the gains are very large or unless an initial innovator believes that he is in a protected position vis-à-vis followers. Thus the usual dilemma that arises will be that in order to get the innovating process started someone has to find himself in a protected position or he must obtain such a position through political, legal, or other means. However, the fact of having a protected position decreases the pressure necessary to maintain X-efficiency. The usual resolution of this dilemma is to offer firms which are potential innovators special *temporary* privileges in the form of patents, copyrights, exclusive licenses, or tax advantages. The difficulty here is that while such techniques do provide the innovators with protection against the impact of followers, they also create a payoff for efforts that extend these protections indefinitely. In other words, it is conceivable that the effort to maintain a sheltered position may be a more profitable return on effort than the effort required to keep X-inefficiency low or to keep it from rising.

Clearly the argument in the previous paragraph depends on the relationship between initiators and followers. It seems self-evident that where there are no followers the initiator is in a superior position, if indeed he does initiate the innovation, than if there are followers. But we have already alluded to the fact that a monopoly position carries with it a very low level of pressure to introduce the innovation unless its introduction is associated with obtaining or retaining the monopoly position. Followers are likely to have two consequences compared to earlier initiators. First, followers put more pressure on everyone to keep X-efficiency low or prevent it from rising. At the same time, since followers can observe some of the adverse experiences and pitfalls experienced by the previous initiators, they reduce the risk of innovation. On the other hand, followers are likely to be forced to innovate in order to protect their relative position in the industry. Hence we see that in general the adoption of an innovation requires simultaneously some advantage to initiators and a significant disadvantage to non-followers, but at the same time a relatively low risk deviation between initiators and followers.

It should be clear from the above discussion of the innovative process that there are many circumstances one could think of under which innovations would not be introduced or would be introduced at a very slow pace. Where the gains from innovating are clearly large, and the risks are low, and followers face no great disadvantage compared to originators, then the innovation will start and spread through the industry. However, there are likely to be a great many cases where the return to the innovation and to potential initiators is not all that large as to overcome all concern about the risks involved. In these cases different economies with different stocks of entrepreneurs and different configurations of inert area bounds may behave quite differently. It is such differences that may help to explain the relatively more rapid rates of growth in some countries or during some periods compared to others.

LOCKED-IN TECHNIQUES, LOCKED-OUT TECHNIQUES, AND X-EFFICIENCY OF LABOR

We shall show in this section that part of the difficulty of capital absorption may arise because in some industries a country may not be in a position to take advantage of the technical knowledge that exists. The reason for this is a mixture of gaps in the types of capital goods produced, even though in principle there is a continuum of such goods that are produceable, and an inability in the country to adapt capital equipment that is imported from abroad but that is entirely unsuitable given the prices of capital and labor in the country in question. This latter problem in part will arise because innovations are likely to be of a localized character. That is to say, improvements in techniques do not take place for all existing techniques but only for a subgroup of such techniques. In general improvements take place for those techniques used in advanced countries and not for those used in the developing countries. This may result in one of two possibilities: a country being *locked-out* of new techniques of production, or a country being *locked-into* other techniques. In the first case certain techniques are not accessible to a country because the improvements take place at relative capital-labor scarcities which are irrelevant to the country in question. In the second case a country is stuck with a certain technique because, if it tries to shift to other techniques, it finds that labor becomes X-inefficient to a sufficient degree as to overcome the advantage of what would be the superior technique if X-inefficiency did not accompany the shift in technique.

We now turn to discuss some of these ideas in greater detail. First notice that localized technological change implies that only a portion of the production function shifts at any one time.

Where switches in technique are concerned, one may distinguish two types of X-inefficiency: the first is transitional X-inefficiency; the second is the comparative degree of X-inefficiency. By transitional X-inefficiency we mean the degree of inefficiency which occurs as the consequence of a technical switch but which is temporary in nature. By switch X-inefficiency we mean the ratio of the degree of X-inefficiency prior to the switch compared to what it is afterwards, inclusive of some allocation of the transition costs involved.

Two factors may account for transitional X-inefficiency: (1) individuals may be committed to traditional work habits or to a traditional work code, and as a result resist work arrangements appropriate for the new technique; (2) if the new technique is expected to decrease employment opportunities for some people, then individuals assigned to it may attempt to use work-spreading tactics.

There are a great many reasons why the degree of X-efficiency should change when there is a change from technique T_1 to T_2, but for our purposes it is not necessary to cover all possibilities. The following reasons might be mentioned. (1) Tastes for different activities may be further from the activity mix that maximizes output under T_2 than under T_1. (2) The degree of coordination and factory discipline required may be greater for the new technique than for the old. (3) The existing technique may be carried out fairly efficiently, but in a highly rigid manner, which may be detrimental to the synchronization of activities required under the new technique. (4) The system of personnel selection appropriate for T_1 may not be suitable for T_2.

(5) The balance of fears and hopes existing in a certain job situation may change when the technique changes, and as a consequence the morale aspects of the work situation may change accordingly. (6) There may be a trade-off between effort and the increase in potential output under T_2 as compared to T_1. If the output standard per person remains constant, then the entire increased productive potential could be taken in less effort. On the other hand, the change to the new technique may suggest a share in the potential rewards of rising productivity and result in a higher effort level than would otherwise be the case. (7) The new technique may require a scale of operations different from the old one, but the skill mix available in the work force may be more appropriate to the smaller scale than to the larger. In general, there is little that can be said as to whether the new technique will be more or less X-efficient than the old one without examining the initial conditions in detail.

A logical complement to the notion of X-efficiency is a somewhat different conception of a production function. One can visualize a production function as a set of "recipes." Each recipe indicates most of the essential elements that enter into the production of the output, but like a real recipe, or a real blueprint, it does not truly indicate all of them. A given recipe may be carried out slowly or quickly or with careful or sloppy workmanship. (After all, different cooks will turn out meals of different quality on the basis of the same recipe.) Since a recipe may involve various amounts of labor in units of time, it would now be illustrated by a segment rather than a point on an isoquant map.

Figure 6.2 illustrates a shift from technique T_1 to technique T_2. We assume that the budget line marked W_2 is consistent with the wage level that would make it worthwhile to shift to T_2. Let us now examine the X-inefficient switch possibility indicated in the figure as T'_2. The budget line tangent at this point will imply a lower wage level. This means that it is less likely for the shift in technique to take place if the wage level were lower than would be the case if the shift were to T_2, under which X-inefficiency does not decrease. Similarly, at the other extreme, the point T_2'' implies an X-efficient shift and is associated with a potentially higher wage level. In this case, the shift would be worthwhile, not only at the existing wage level W_2, but even if the wage level rose.

A point on an isoquant no longer represents a technique, in the sense of a given recipe. Since any recipe can be related to varying quantities of labor to produce a certain output, a given

Figure 6.2 X-efficient and X-inefficient switches in techniques

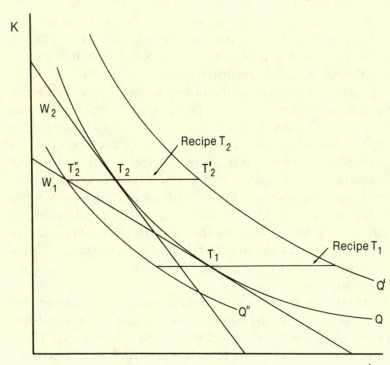

$Q' = $ X-inefficient bound
$Q = $ Equi-X-efficient isoquant

technique is represented by *at least* a line segment. If techniques are continuous, the segments are continuous, and the isoquant is no longer a line but an area of varying degrees of thickness. There is significance, however, in an isoquant of the usual kind where a single point represents a technique, if we allow every point to represent the same degree of X-efficiency. A shift involving an increase in X-efficiency means a movement to a lower "equi-X-efficient" isoquant, and vice versa. Thus, for a given rate of wage increase, a firm will move more rapidly to more capital intensive techniques the greater the degree of X-efficiency associated with such techniques. Indeed, when there are discontinuities in technique, we may expect slow changes if the move is X-inefficient and more rapid ones if technique switches are X-efficient.

In the simplified case considered here, every technique (or "recipe") is associated with a unique amount of capital but a variable quantity of labor. Hence, every technique is represented by a line segment parallel to the labor axis. We shall not consider the more likely situation in which somewhat variable amounts of capital may also be associated with a given recipe. It seems reasonable to presume that a given recipe need not specify the amount of capital with complete precision. Wastefulness in the use of capital is certainly possible and likely. Under such circumstances each recipe then becomes a sausage-shaped area in a two-dimensional diagram. The integral of such overlapping areas will then become a given isoquant. For present purposes we will ignore the implications of this version of the production function.

In general, an increase in X-efficiency operates in a way similar to learning by doing. Furthermore, switches could be X-inefficient while there is no negative "learning by doing." Hence, a firm contemplating a shift in technique must take into account not only the change in the relative prices of inputs but also the degree to which the change will be X-efficient or X-inefficient. For instance, in figure 6.2 the change illustrated by the new wage rate W_2 would not be worthwhile if the switch in technique was X-inefficient.

As in learning by doing, changes in X-efficiency may involve externalities. An innovation may pay even though it is X-inefficient, but if these X-inefficiencies spread to other firms because of the new but more slack standards of work in the innovating firm, then the social cost of the innovation will be greater than its direct private cost, and the innovation may not pay from a social viewpoint though it may appear to do so from a private one. Or, the introduction of an X-efficient technical change in some firms may raise the quality-effort standard and make efficient labor available to other firms. The policy implications of such an effect is that governments should encourage (subsidize) those technological changes which exhibit X-efficient external benefits and should tax those whose externalities are X-inefficient.

A lack of technological change, or a slow rate of such change, may be explained to some degree by whether or not (and the extent to which) such changes are accompanied by improvements in X-efficiency. Firms and economies whose alternative technical options are X-inefficient may choose not to introduce them, or if they do, they will discover them to be uneconomic and abandon them.

The main consideration to be kept in mind is the possibility that an industry may be *locked-in* on a given technique if the shift in the direction required for adjustment is X-inefficient. Similarly, technological changes may not be introduced if such changes are localized and X-inefficient. The basic idea is elementary. The loss from the X-inefficiency accompanying the change may be greater than the benefit that would otherwise have occurred as a consequence of the change. The implications of this possibility may be of considerable importance. For a given range of change in some variable (e.g., the wage rate), changes that would take place in response to a disequilibrium state may in fact not occur. This "locked-in technique" concept may help to explain certain types of phenomena familiar in less developed countries.

Suppose that all innovations are visualized in terms of borrowing new recipes from more advanced countries and substituting them for some of the existing recipes. Suppose further that a new recipe is understood only to the extent to which it is reasonably close to an existing one. It will obviously make a difference whether the new recipes available are many or few compared to those currently in use. Thus, if research and technological change take place mostly in advanced countries, this would imply that new recipes are created in relatively high capital/labor ratio countries and are not generally available in the relatively low capital/labor ratio countries.

We can readily think of countries as being located in different positions in technological space. The chief consideration for the technology borrowing country is how far or how close it is in technological space to the lending countries and at what point in technological space are inventions (i.e., new recipes) being made.

Thus countries which find themselves in technological space at the relatively low capital/labor ratio end may also find that they have relatively few new recipes available to them for borrowing. Clearly their experience will be disappointing if in addition the few recipes they can borrow are X-inefficient in implementation. We may visualize this as a situation which involves being *locked-out* from technological options that may be available in other economies.

This idea (which explains a possibility but not necessarily the *only* source of relative technological stagnation) is illustrated in figure 6.3 where points representing high capital/labor ratios are shown to follow a path of localized and X-efficient innovations T_2 and T_3, while those with a low capital/labor ratios yield localized and X-inefficient innovations T'_2 and T'_3 (or no innovations at all). Under such circumstances low income countries would be technologically stagnant, while high income ones

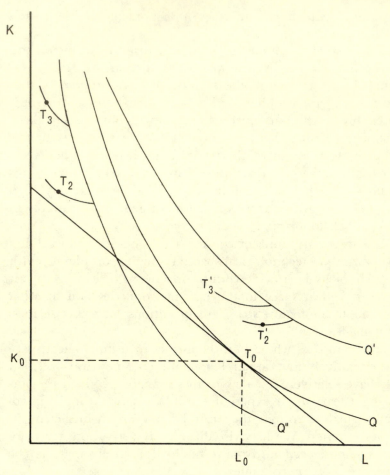

Figure 6.3 Innovational diffusion and technological stagnation

would show continued technological change. The borrowing country at position T_0 cannot benefit from the inventions T_2 and T_3 taking place in the lending country.

Or consider the following possibility. We start with a pair of economies A and B which are similar in almost every respect.

The same rate of investment exists in both. Part of the investment is spent for capital widening and capital deepening, while
another part is spent for the introduction of technological
change. Suppose that in country A technological change is
X-efficient while in B it is X-inefficient, though entrepreneurs
in both countries expect the degree of X-efficiency to remain un-
changed. In A the results will more than justify expectations
in terms of output and profit, while in B the opposite will be
the case. As a consequence A shifts more of its investment funds
into technological change, while B moves in the opposite direction.

In a locked-out technique new techniques cannot be reached
because improvements are taking place in a relatively distant
portion of the technological space. As a result the industry has
to wait until it advances sufficiently so that it becomes economic
to adopt and adapt the innovations available elsewhere.

A locked-in technique involves a different type of problem.
Superior techniques are available within the technological
space that the industry occupies. The difficulty arises because
adopting a new technique results simultaneously in an increase
in X-inefficiency of the labor component. This is shown in figure 6.4 if we assume that the actual labor required will be the
outer bound of the isoquant shown by Q^*. As usual each recipe
is associated with various amounts of labor but the outer bound
is what is actually anticipated. Hence, the isoquant which is
normally concave from the origin takes on a convex component
and points in this component are not reachable in terms of the
normal prices for capital and labor. Of course the diagram only
illustrates the consequences of X-inefficiency and cannot indicate why this should be the case. In general we should expect
that there is an organizational deficiency which is somehow responsible for the problem. In other words, the new techniques
require somewhat different forms of organizing the work in the
industry in question so that, with given organizational capacities that happen to be available to the industry in question, the

use of labor becomes more X-inefficient with the new technique. A possibility may be that the new technique requires a larger scale of operation which in turn results in the less efficient utilization of labor.

Whatever the detailed reasons for either locked-in or locked-out techniques, we can see that these concepts allow us to get an analytical handle on some of the possible sources of the inability for capital absorption that frequently exists in developing countries.

Figure 6.4

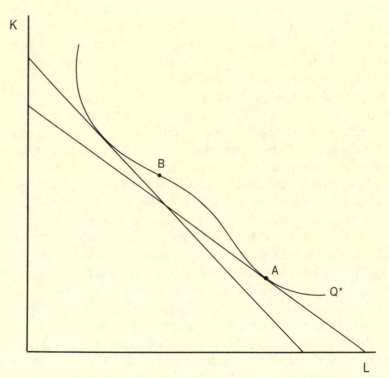

$AB = A$ "locked-in" technique area

Population Growth and the Economic Theory of Fertility

POPULATION GROWTH AND FERTILITY

Population growth frequently puts pressure on attempts to increase per capita income growth. To start with, we should keep in mind that per capita income growth is the difference between aggregate income growth and population growth. Thus, if there are enough resources for growth, and the aggregate income growth is 4% and population growth is 3%, the per capita growth rate falls to 1%. In most developing countries population growth rates are between 1.5% and 3.5%. The range of aggregate economic growth rates is, of course, much wider, but the average, even in years of relatively rapid growth, is between 4% and 5%. On this basis alone the relative significance of population growth should be apparent. But it should also be apparent that in most cases population growth is not an insurmountable obstacle to achieving some steady per capita income growth. A great deal depends on how the pressures that population growth engenders in various sectors of the economy work themselves out.

The immediate economic effects of population growth are that it (1) tends to increase the burden of dependency of the working population and (2) it may possibly drain off or reduce

123

what little household savings would otherwise take place. In the long run, population growth determines the rate of labor force growth in various sectors. We have already discussed in previous chapters the various pressures that labor force may engender. Within agriculture it is one of the main factors that decreases arable land availability per worker and helps to explain the existence of actual or disguised unemployment within that sector. At the same time, it stimulates the level of net rural-urban migration. The movement of workers to urban areas, plus labor force growth within the urban sector creates the type of employment absorption problems discussed earlier. To complete the picture we shall see in this chapter that rural-urban migration is a major force in stimulating the reduction in fertility rates, which in turn sometimes reduces the rate of population growth almost to zero, as a country approaches a high level of development.

Population growth is determined essentially by mortality and fertility rates (assuming, as is customary in such analysis, that we abstract from international migration). Prior to World War II it was probably reasonable to presume that mortality rates were closely tied to changes in general economic conditions. Since then the availability of inexpensive public health measures has led to a situation under which relatively low mortality rates can be achieved almost in the absence of increases in economic growth. Despite the fact that economic growth still plays a role in reducing mortality, it is probably no longer the major factor. Hence, it seems reasonable at this stage to focus our attention on changes in fertility in order to help us understand the factors which cause changes in population growth.

In general, fertility rates are high in developing countries, especially in the early stages of per capita income growth. As the process of economic development proceeds, one of two patterns is likely to emerge: (1) either fertility rises for a while and then sustained decline sets in or (2) fertility fluctuates around a relatively high constant level and then sustained fertility declines set in. In any event, the major general phenomenon to be explained is why sustained economic growth should be associated with the eventual decline in fertility. This will be our main concern in this chapter.

Two types of arguments are frequently presented against an economic theory of fertility. (1) People in developing countries do not use modern contraceptive means. (2) Fertility behavior is culturally determined, and hence it is not determined by the private economic calculation of the parents.

We dwell briefly on the first point. High fertility rates in underdeveloped countries are considerably below their biological maximum—probably 40%–60% below the Hutterite level.[1] Therefore, even in instances where fertility is traditionally high, a wide variety of traditional child spacing and family size controls are practiced—deferred marriage, abortions, taboos on sexual intercourse, long periods of lactation, coitus interruptus, etc. One need not specify all possible means. Many of the countries that achieved their fertility decline earlier did so prior to the widespread distribution of modern contraceptive practices. Furthermore, all means of population control are substitutes to some degree for other means.

For an economic theory to be valid, one need not assume that *typical* behavior is "rational." It is sufficient that behavior at critical junctures be "rational." Only selective rationality need be operative. Assume that the age of marriage and the birth of the final child depend on calculated considerations, although all intervening fertility behavior is "spontaneous." Under these conditions *average* typical behavior appears to be nonrational, but marginal behavior is rational. If the start-stop points are determined by "calculation," then family size is determined, despite the fact that spacing will have a random component—or, follows traditional behavior.

Although *marginal* behavior is "rational," it need not be cal-

[1] United Nations, Department of Economic and Social Affairs, *Demographic Yearbook, 1969* (New York: International Publications Service, 1970), pp. 222–34. See also T. J. Eaton and A. J. Mayer, "The Social Biology of Very High Fertility Among the Hutterites," *Human Biology* 25 (September 1953): 206–64.

culated in a narrow sense. In conformity with selective rationality theory, it may be a response to the buildup of sufficient economic pressure. That is, economic pressure leads to sufficient
constraint concern so that a marginal decision is made of the
type that would be made *approximately* if more careful calculation had taken place. On the other hand, allowing for the
buildup of economic pressure to determine the fertility decision may lead to delay in the imposition of constraint concern
so that the end result is one in which the family ends up with
slightly more children than it really wants. This last situation is
consistent with survey data available from developing countries. In other words, people frequently report having somewhat
more children than desired.

Throughout the rest of this chapter, where in the interests
of brevity we seem to suggest careful calculation, the reader
should keep in mind the possibility of reinterpreting the theory
in the manner we have just indicated. Our strategy in this
chapter is not to interpret everything in terms of selective rationality theory. In the interests of brevity a compromise is attempted. Elements of selective rationality theory will be introduced at various junctures in the hope that it may illuminate
our discussion of the nature of the process of fertility decline.[2]

2 This chapter is motivated in part by the belief that, if a population has homoge-
nous tastes (i.e., not dependent on status or "lifestyle"), it is implausible for the
cost of children, especially those attributed to "quality" or mother's time (as
argued by the Chicago school), to account for the frequently found inverse relation between family size and income level, given the income growth that occurs
in the course of development. That is, sustained income increases over time must
enable families to afford larger numbers of children at previous standard of child
nurture. Something must change drastically if fewer children are desired at
higher incomes. The alternative that we shall employ is to view populations as
composed of social status groups that have different tastes, and who especially see
the whole cost structure of their expenditures, including expenditures for children, from the viewpoint of vastly different preference structures. Groups other
than socioeconomic groups may be more important at different stages in the development process. In some cases caste or religion or ethnic groupings may appear
more significant than socioeconomic groups. Population movements between
groups will change preferences of those that move. The foregoing remarks should

In the pages that follow we shall first try to show that there is good reason for the cost of children to rise significantly as we proceed from lower social status groups to higher ones and as per capita group increases in the course of economic development. In later schemes we will consider also changes in the satisfaction derived from children as economic development takes place.

DEVELOPMENT, STATUS SHIFTS, AND INCOME COMPRESSION EFFECTS

Fertility is significantly influenced by events that accompany economic development. We present a brief stylized view of the development process and consider its impact. Basic to the development process is a persistent shift of labor (and households) out of agriculture into urban pursuits so that the ratio in agriculture changes from over 80% of the population to less than 20%. In general, the labor force shifts into manufacturing up to a maximum of 35%, while the rest moves into nonrural tertiary pursuits that include a vast variety of services such as trade, banking, and transportation.[3] These labor force shifts are associated with increases in education per worker, on-the-job training, and with a considerable increase in the amount of human capital per worker and per household member. Also, the work force becomes more highly differentiated in terms of (1) occupation, (2) skill content or education, and (3) assets per household—all of which are likely to be indices of status.

We shall emphasize two aspects of the process of urbaniza-

---

not be taken to imply that the direct and indirect costs of children are not important, or that they are not likely to be higher in higher income groups than in lower ones. However, they are not sufficient to carry the weight of the entire decision process.

3 See P. Bairoch and J. M. Limbor, "Changes in the Industrial Distribution of the World Labour Force, by Region, 1880–1960," *Essays on Employment*, ed. Walter Galenson (Geneva: International Labour Office, 1971), especially pp. 34–40, for a summary of the relevant data.

tion and occupational shift: (1) the shift of greater proportions of the population into higher socioeconomic statuses than would have been the case had the country remained at its lower income level and (2) the simultaneous growth of per capita income. We shall argue that while *both* of these factors influence the *utility* attached to children and the *utility* of the typical expenditure patterns of households, which in turn determine the *utility costs* associated with children, the status-shift effects and income effects play very different roles. They may even affect fertility in opposite ways.

We live in social groups. Beyond basic sustenance, consumption has a broad social status (lifestyle) basis. In our analysis we distinguish ordinary consumption expenditures from *status* (or lifestyle) goods expenditures. The household's view of status depends on a reference group of "important others" who influence the consumption decisions of the household. The utility of such expenditures is in part a reflection of expectations of explicit or implicit approval or disapproval of the important others.

For present purposes status depends on (1) occupation, (2) education, and (3) consumer durable assets. We assume a status hierarchy. A household in a higher status is not always associated with a higher income, although the mean income for a higher status group is usually higher than that of a lower one. For ease of exposition consider a three-status, two-period model as illustrated in table 7.1. The two periods may be viewed as approximately fifteen years apart. The numbers in column (*4*) compared to those in column (*1*) illustrate the interstatus-income ratio compression effect.[4] This is a well-documented, almost

---

[4] See Harold Lydall, *The Structure of Earnings* (London: Oxford University Press, 1968), pp. 163–99. See also Simon Kuznets, "Economic Growth and Income Inequality," *American Economic Review* 45 (March 1955): 1–28. Kuznets indicates that income distribution is likely to become more unequal in the earlier stages of development as the high-productivity industrial sector expands relative to the low-productivity agricultural sector, but that in the later stages of development income becomes more equally distributed.

Table 7.1

| | | Period 1 | | | Period 2 | |
| | | Status expenditures | Nonstatus expenditures | | Status expenditures | Nonstatus expenditures |
Status	Income (1)	(2)	(3)	Income (4)	(5)	(6)
(Lowest) 1	100	40	60	200	100	100
2	200	100	100	300	210	90
3	300	150	150	350	300	50

universal phenomenon that has been studied extensively by labor economists. For example, in a developing country an engineer might earn twenty times the income of an agricultural laborer, while in a high-income country the ratio might be reduced to three.

We assume that the income distribution remains more or less constant. If households move disproportionately to higher statuses between two periods, and simultaneously interstatus-income ratios fall, then it is possible to retain the same income distribution. Now, consider some of the possible consequences of relative income compression on the basis of the following reasonable hypotheses: (1) Families have a strong desire to avoid a fall in status. (2) Some families will want to emulate those in higher statuses for themselves or for their children. (3) Services are disproportionately involved in "status goods." The higher the status, the greater the expenditure on status goods that involve services. Since the general wage rises, we expect services to be more expensive in period 2 than in period 1. For example, educational costs would probably rise between the two periods. (4) Families try to maintain a strong status differential through their expenditure patterns. To start, assume that households attempt to keep the relative expenditures on status goods in the same proportion.

The four hypotheses lead to the conclusion that if status

goods are a significant portion of income, then a considerable squeeze on the proportion of the budget spent on ordinary goods takes place. If those in status-1 consume the same amount of status goods in the second period as was consumed by status-2 families in the first period, and if the differential is maintained, then status-2 families have to double their expenditures on status goods. If previously they spent 50% of their income ($100) on status goods, they will now have to spend twice as much. If, in addition, the price of status goods rises because services cost more, then an even higher proportion has to be spent on status goods. A lower proportion is thus available for non-status expenditures. We shall argue that to the extent there is a utility cost of children that is distinct for each status, the utility foregone for an nth-order child–*could* be higher in a higher status than in a lower one.

STATUS GOODS, COMMITMENT GOODS,
AND OTHER IMU GOODS

A critical part of our analysis is based on a variant of the theory of consumer behavior that differs from conventional theory. We posit the existence of goods that are subject to *increasing* marginal utility up to some level and to normal diminishing marginal utility beyond that level. As a shorthand we refer to these as IMU goods. We distinguish four possible characteristics of such goods: (1) consumer durables subject to physical indivisibilities or significant economies of scale, (2) what we shall call "commitment" goods, (3) status or "lifestyle" goods, and (4) "target goods" in the sense that there is some target quantity or expenditure that is especially significant for some reason and anything less than the target amount is of little utility. These characteristics are not distinct. Some expenditures may fall into all four categories, others may not.

Consider the following example. Suppose that someone takes a foreign language given in monthly units. After six months he can receive certification indicating a certain level of proficiency useful for normal conversation. The person may feel that any number of lessons are useful but that hitting the minimal conversational proficiency level is especially important. For such a person the marginal utility of each lesson increases until the critical proficiency level (his target) is reached. Beyond that point diminishing marginal utility sets in. The person is "committed" to a certain minimum expenditure. We shall argue that by and large status maintenance expenditures are commitment goods in the sense indicated, although some may not be of this type.

An important analytical possibility is that the utility for some set of goods depends on the deviation from some set of accepted consumption "norms." In other words, what matters, at least in part, is the relative consumption level rather than the absolute level. Certain classes of consumption may be related to such psychological magnitudes as the sense of self-esteem or significance, or of attainment, etc., so that comparison with others is the critical criterion that scores. The basic idea is illustrated in figure 7.1. We show marginal utility per dollar spent (price is given) on the ordinate and expenditures on the abscissa. (This is indicated by MU in figure 7.1.) q^* is the class norm. We can readily imagine that there may be consumption or expenditures for which people feel that they would like to reach or exceed the class norms. Utility rises rapidly until the point at which the class norm is reached, although the highest marginal utility may be at a point greater than the class norm, say at q_0. In other words, the optimal quantity from a comparative viewpoint is larger than the class norm by a given degree.

An important type of *commitment*, which occurs especially in higher statuses and increases with status, is the provision for old-age security. This is frequently looked upon as one of the utilities for children, but for higher income groups it could be viewed as a significant expense. Clearly, the amount of provision for old-age security depends on the life style one is used to and

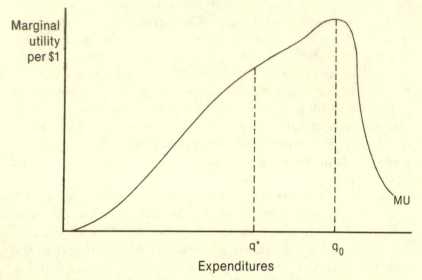

Figure 7.1

hence also the life style one aims at during old age. Thus, this commitment component operates in the same way as the status or IMU goods would operate.[5]

Expenditures on commitment goods are different from ordinary expenditures in the same sense that long-run costs differ

[5] Ronald Freedman points out the degree to which old-age security may have influenced the falling Japanese birth rate. He writes: "Recent Japanese data provide a striking illustration of the close relation between norms about dependence on adult children and the course of fertility. Between 1950 and 1961 the Japanese birth rate fell spectacularly from 28 to 17 per 1000. In the same period the biennial sample surveys by the Mainichi press posed to a representative cross-section of the population the question: 'Do you expect to depend on your children in your old age?' In 1950 a majority, more than 55 percent, answered 'definitely yes.' The proportion giving this answer declined steadily in five succeeding surveys, reaching 27 percent by 1961. It is rare that public opinion on a matter this vital changes so steadily and rapidly and just as rare that we have statistical data with which to document the trend" (Ronald Freedman, "Norms for Family Size in Underdeveloped Areas," *Population and Society*, ed. Charles B. Nam [Boston: Houghton Mifflin Company, 1968], p. 222).

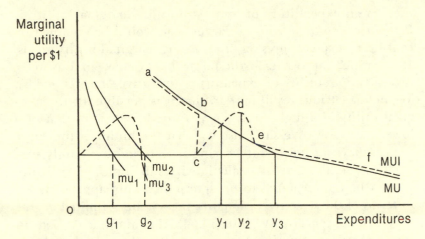

Figure 7.2

from short-run costs. Once the commitment is made, it contin-
ues for some period of time, even if "tastes" change. Thus, some
expenditures on children, or on other household members, involve *minimal* commitments that do *not* reflect tastes, but reflect
the *fact* of the long-term responsibility involved in the child-
parent relation, or family relations, thus determining expenditure *commitments* associated with a particular status.

We now turn to show the significance of IMU goods on the
marginal utility of income. In figure 7.2 mu_1 and mu_2 are the
marginal utility curves for ordinary goods 1, 2, etc. prices are
given). Suppose that only ordinary goods existed. Then MU,
the lateral summation of the curves mu_i, for all i, is the marginal
utility of income curve. (Of course, these curves are for *only* one
set of prices. The curves have to be redrawn for each price
change.)

Now consider what happens when we introduce the IMU
good shown by the broken line mu_3. As we proceed down our
marginal expenditure function, we can no longer proceed by
marginal dollars spent. At each point we must ask whether

there is an expenditure of some size whose marginal utility is low but whose *total utility* is larger than would be obtained by continuing expenditures on diminishing marginal utility goods. In figure 7.2 this occurs at the point b. The new curve is MUI (i.e., marginal utility of expenditures inclusive of IMU goods). We note a curious result here in that it is possible for the marginal utility of a higher income y_2 to be higher than that of a lower income y_1. We shall also see that the hump in the curve *cde* can have an important bearing in determining family size.

Of course, the carefully calculated result indicated in figure 7.2 can be reinterpreted to be determined only approximately in terms of the selective rationality theory and a limited degree of constraint concern. We interpret IMU commitment goods in terms of selective rationality theory. In other words, certain types of purchasing behavior, such as keeping up with others in one's social group, is an inert area phenomenon. That is, the household makes what appear to be socially required expenditures. It is only when such expenditures get beyond certain boundaries that constraint concern takes hold and pressure forces "calculated" changes.

COMMITMENT CLAIM GROWTH

In previous sections we treated the household as a unit. However, in order to see how pressures accumulate to maintain (or pursue) status through the purchase of status goods, it is useful to examine the processes of *intra*household claims, whether implicit, subdued, or explicit and to consider the interactions of *intra*household claim compromises among family members and *inter*household emulation through demographically similar individuals. In accordance with selective rationality theory, we stress at this point the relation between individual decision making within the household and household decisions.

As family income increases claims by family members on household, income is likely to increase. Three elements likely to play a role are (1) the nature of the resolution of conflicting claims prior to the income increase, (2) the degree to which the other households in the same "social influence group" (SIG) have also had income growth, (3) competitive appeals for fairness. We shall consider claim pressures from the viewpoint of the net contributor (one of the parents) and refer to others in the household as claimants.

Whatever the scheme of distribution of household income, it seems reasonable that as income increases claimants should want more spent on them. The elements that are likely to determine the outcome of additional claims are (1) expenditure control, (2) the quantity of expenditures, and (3) the imposition of negative affect. That is, the parent who is the net contributor may want some control over the nature of the expenditure. Usually, this parent will want to know if the claim of some particular family member is for a "reasonable" purpose. Of course, the claimant wants to minimize control. At the same time, the claimant can impose negative affect (reduction of love, increased anger, etc.) as a counter to the ultimate power over income that may reside in the hands of the net contributor parent. In any event, we see that there are possible trade-offs between control, the increase in the quantity of the expenditure on the claimants and changes in affect, which can be used to obtain a compromise solution. In the absence of a compromise solution, the will of the net contributor would have to be imposed at the price of the negative affect that results.

In many cases unwelcome compromises may have to be imposed on at least some family members, since all must ultimately yield to the income constraint. It is as though the net contributor has built a dike to dam the wave of claims. But the dike may overflow once the potential claimants perceive an increase in income. Claimants rush to renegotiate. The net contributor may find it hard to struggle against the onslaught, especially since in some cases some family members may aspire to a higher social status in making their claims. We must keep in mind the asymmetry that exists in this connection—many aspire upwards, but few aspire to a fall in status.

If we define total claim elasticity as the ratio of the increase in all claims to the increase in income, then claim elasticity in the previous case is most likely greater than unity. Consider especially the case in which all households in a given social influence group (SIG)[6] receive an increase in income. Once the family agrees to live in a style somewhat similar to those who are in its SIG, many areas of discretion are narrowed. Family members with similar demographic characteristics (age, sex, etc.) will to some extent have to be equipped with similar material goods. Furthermore, the example set by expenditures in other households of demographically similar family members will be used in appeals to "fairness." If such appeals are met in different households, the expenditure per family member rises, creating grounds for still further appeals for higher expenditures, to the point at which pressure is exerted toward the absorption of the entire income increase by claimants. The very meaning of belonging (and, especially, *demonstrating* belonging) to a given SIG implies some similarity in the type of expenditure patterns.

Not receiving appropriate commitment toward a claimant may be viewed as questioning whether the parents in control are living up to the image of the particular SIG to which they directly or indirectly claim to belong. The process of competition between households and between demographically similar household members puts pressures on those who control household income to treat their own members no worse than they are treated in other approximately similarly placed households.

In general, we should expect that the proportion of household income that goes to all commitments rises with increases in socioeconomic status. The reason for this is that to a consid-

---

[6] The term SIG and social status group will be used interchangeably. The appropriate social influence groups may differ considerably in different cultures. Hence, in doing empirical work in order to test this theory, identifying the appropriate social influence groups, or optimal proxies for such groups, may be a very important and distinct aspects of the empirical problem.

erable degree one needs either to be a commitment recipient or to have a fairly high income before one can safely and easily become a commitment payer. There is a necessary relationship between the steadiness of income receipts (or the level of permanent income) to the household and its ability to supply commitments. In the world of the day laborer receiving an irregular wage, there are likely to be many fewer commitments to household members (or outsiders) than in the world of the professional receiving an annual salary. In brief, a relatively stable income stream to the household permits the household to undertake stable commitments to both household members and outsiders, and this capacity increases as we go up the socioeconomic scale. In the course of economic development, job formalization and professionalization increase, which in turn increase the ability of all groups to grant commitments.

Suppose for a moment that the marginal income elasticities of claims and of commitments for a group of households are greater than unity. The lower the household income within a socioeconomic status group and the lower the *increase* in income, the greater the marginal elasticities. One can see that in this case the absolute amount left to net contributors (one or both parents) may be no greater than before the income increases. To the extent that this type of intrahousehold pressure builds up, one can readily see that an increase in household income (when other incomes rise simultaneously) will not yield much of a decrease in pressure. In fact for many households this will produce an increase in pressure to grant commitments to family members to maintain or pursue status, and to enter into commitments with outsiders so that, on balance, the portion of the anticipated income stream left for family size expansion may be proportionately or absolutely less than before.

INTERSTATUS UTILITY DIFFERENTIALS AND THE COST OF CHILDREN

It seems intuitively plausible, but impossible to prove, that if a higher status person had the same income as a lower status one (not necessarily the same assets), a marginal dollar to a higher status person would have less utility than to a lower one if all goods were ordinary (not IMU goods). In what follows, this will be the assumption we shall use.

We now introduce the concept of *average equal utility expenditure units* (to be referred to as AEU units). Suppose that the total utility of the higher status person is one and one half times that of the lower status person. We then compute what would be the equivalent number of dollars for a higher status person that would yield the same utility as one dollar for a lower status one. This enables us to use average equal utility expenditure units to compare the decisions of higher status and lower status households. Let y_1 and y_2 be the incomes for the two households, and TU_1 and TU_2 their total utilities. Then an AEU unit is defined as the one which sets:

$$\frac{y_2}{TU_2} = \frac{y_1}{TU_1}$$

For instance, if incomes are $300 in the higher status household and $100 in the lower one and total utilities are 200 for the higher income and 100 for the lower one, then an AEU unit will represent $1.50 for the higher income and $1 for the lower income.

In figure 7.3 the abscissa indicates the equivalent utility expenditure units. The ordinate represents marginal utility. We assume that for AEU units, marginal utility falls just as rapidly for higher status individuals as it does for lower status individuals. We can easily relax this assumption to obtain similar results, but that would only complicate the exposition unnecessarily.

The curve MUE is the marginal utility of expenditures (in AEU units) for the two households. The curves marked UV_1 and UV_2 are the utility values of children for the lower and higher status respectively. We read the utility value of marginal children from right to left as indicated by the arrow. The area

adx_1y_1 represents the utility value of a first child in the household in status 1. We assume that in terms of AEU units the utility value of an nth-order child is the same. The arbitrarily assumed equal distances,[7] y_2y_1, y_1x_1, x_1x_2, etc., are the average utility costs of children in terms of equi-utility expenditure units. As a first step we assume that the cost of child rearing is the same for the two groups in AEU units. Of course, this means that in dollars it is higher for the higher status.

We can now read off the results in figure 7.3. The first point

[7] Equality of distances is assumed for ease in exposition only. A more realistic figure would show the cost of the first child about twice the size of the second, but subsequent distances could be approximately equal or declining somewhat. See Thomas J. Espenshade, "Estimating the Cost of Children and Some Results from Urban United States," Preliminary Paper No. 4, February 1973, International Population and Urban Research, University of California, Berkeley, pp. 15ff.

Figure 7.3

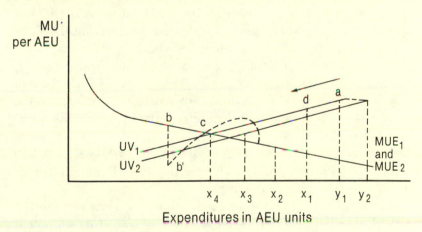

Expenditures in AEU units

AEU = Average equi-utility units
MUE = Marginal utility of expenditure curve for both individuals
y_1 = Income for status 1
y_2 = Income for status 2
UV_1 = Marginal utility for children in AEU units for status 1
UV_2 = Marginal utility for children in AEU units for status 2

to observe is that, if all goods were ordinary goods, the family size for the higher status household would be larger than for the lower status household. This can be seen by comparing the equilibrium points at which the relevant MUE and UV curves intersect. As drawn, the higher status household would have 4.5 children, and the lower status one only 4 children. It is noteworthy, once we introduce status goods (i.e., IMU goods), that the situation reverses itself. We see that the lower status household chooses four children, while the higher one would choose three children. The higher status MUE curve has the "status-goods' IMU hump," which raises the marginal utility cost of children for higher status households. In other words, a fourth child will mean sacrificing the high-status-goods utility. Thus, in the case illustrated, a larger family could threaten the status position of the higher status household.[8]

Now let us relax for a moment the assumption that children in each status cost the same in terms of equi-utility expenditure units. Suppose they cost more in the AEU units for the higher status. Clearly, in this case the qualitative result is similar. The higher status would have even fewer children than otherwise. The situation is more complex if for the higher status there is a lower average expenditure cost in AEU units per child. In that case whether or not the situation reverses itself (compared to the no-status-goods assumption) depends on the degree of the lower cost for the higher status. Thus, while we cannot prove necessarily that higher status (and higher income) households will have fewer children, we show the possibility and argue the probability that this will be the case.

Given the relative status income compression phenomenon, it would appear likely that, even if at the outset of development higher status family size were the same as lower status size, the relative income compression and its impact on status-IMU ex-

---

[8] We can introduce a small-status-good hump on the MUE curve, say between the points b' and c without changing our conclusions. The main point is that the higher status will spend a higher proportion on status-IMU goods.

penditures would eventually lead to a fall in family size for the higher status household.[9]

These basic ideas can also be reinterpreted from a somewhat different viewpoint. We assume that the status expenditures fall into inert areas. Hence what is left, and what is adjustable against other cost considerations, is household income minus the status expenditures. In figure 7.4, we show two curves which indicate the trade-offs between fertility and the income left over. The appropriate indifference curves are also shown in the figure in the usual manner. We notice that for the lower children-income trade-off curve the intercept on the children axis is higher than for the higher income curve. This implies that at the higher income the costs of children are sufficiently larger, so that fewer children are obtainable if all leftover income were spent on children. This may arise for two reasons. It is possible, but not necessary, that the absolute amount of income left over may be lower for the higher income. In other words, status expenditures increase in absolute amount to a greater degree than the increase in income. On the other hand, this last need not be the case. Child nurture costs are sufficiently higher for the higher income group to achieve this result, as shown in the figure. While this increase in nurture costs may be insignificant with regard to the total income for the higher income group, it may prove to be very important compared to the income left

---

9 The relatively rich within a status will have approximately the same utilities and utility costs as the average household in the status, but a lesser budget constraint, and hence will be able to afford and desire more children than the representative household. Hence, birth rates are positively associated with income *within* a status, but not *between* statuses. This is consistent with Deborah Freedman's findings for the United States. See Deborah Freedman, "The Relation of Economic Status to Fertility," *American Economic Review* 53 (June 1963): 414–26. See also Eva M. Bernhardt, "Fertility and Economic Status—Some Recent Findings on Differentials in Sweden," *Population Studies* 26 (July 1972): 175–84. For some occupations, very low-income groups in the occupation have relatively higher fertility rates. This may be because (1) occupation by itself is a poor proxy for status and (2) income (or characteristics that vary with income) is also part of the defining characteristic of status.

over after the inert area determined status expenditures. As a result, in figure 7.4, the number of children per family turns out to be lower for the higher income group.

ON THE UTILITY OF CHILDREN

It will facilitate discussion if we divide the desire for children into three categories—low, medium, and high parity. By low parity we have in mind zero to three children, medium parity represents four to six children, and high parity will represent seven or more children. We have argued in the previous section almost entirely on the basis of utility cost considerations. A question that arises is whether the significant variable is not the utility *value,* so that the entire explanation could be based on a decline of the utility value (benefits) of children as we move from lower to higher statuses and as per capita income increases.

Now the hypothesis we will argue is that, while the utility and desire for high-parity children unquestionably decline in the course of development, the utility and desire for medium-parity children are probably *not* very much lower. As a consequence what has to be explained is how economic costs induce a reduction in actual family size from the medium parity that would be desired to the low parities that actually occur. Some empirical evidence buttressed by theoretical considerations suggest that a plausible argument could be made that the desire for children would not have declined beyond the high middle parities, say 4.5 to 5 children, were it not for the utility costs. Thus, we shall want to show that, while there is reason to believe that the value of high-parity children has declined, there is very little reason to assume this for low- and middle-parity children. In an interesting experiment reported on by Namboodiri,[10] it was

[10] See N. Krishnan Namboodiri, "Some Observations on the Economic Framework for Fertility Analysis," *Population Studies* 26 (July 1972): 185ff. This is based on a pilot study in North Carolina where the income range of the two middle categories was between $7,000 and $13,000 per year. Other studies show similar results.

found that people with relatively low family size, when asked their ideal family size if they had all the income necessary to support any number of children, wanted between 4 and 5 children.

We now consider some of the specifics involved in the utility value of children. Consumption utility reflects the extent to which parents want children as sources of personal satisfaction. How this utility varies with status increase or with income growth is difficult to say. We are concerned only with the utility or a third or higher parity child. As income increases, there are increasingly available alternative sources of satisfaction that are potential substitutes for the consumption utility of high-parity children. However, not to bias the theory unduly, we shall assume that consumption utility is constant or does not fall significantly with respect to status increases or income increases.

A significant sociological concomitant of development is the attenuation and eventual disappearance of the extended family system, in the sense of a kinship system in which there are exceedingly strong bonds of mutual obligation and support. Sociologists have emphasized the extended family as a significant instrument in establishing and maintaining large family norms. The following quotations summarize the essence of the argument.

In most preindustrial societies a wide range of activities involve interdependence with kinsmen. . . . These include production, consumption, leisure activity, assistance in illness and old age and many other activities covered by non-familial institutions in modern societies. To simplify greatly: large numbers of children are desired if the values considered worthwhile are obtained through familial ties rather than through other social institutions. . . . This, in turn, depends on the division of labor between the family and other social institutions and on how much the performance of important functions by the family depends on the number of children produced in it.[11]

11 Ronald Freedman, "Norms for Family Size in Underdeveloped Areas," *Population and Society*, ed. Charles B. Nam (Boston: Houghton Mifflin Company, 1968), pp. 220–21.

Islam partakes of the pro-natalist social forces that exist generally in peasant and pastoral societies. . . . Sons are valued for many purposes: for continuity of family line and land-ownership; for contribution to agricultural labor; to strengthen family numbers in village rivalry and strife; for support in old age; for religious intervention at and after death. As in other developing societies . . . , the joint family system in Islam buffers the direct burdens of childbearing on the parents.[12]

It seems natural to give these notions an economic interpretation. The extended family system is an arrangement whereby the kinship group provides an informal trading system of desired *services* for its members through a system of mutual obligation. Among these services are insurance against economic disaster, insurance against the consequences of some children not working out well, old-age security, and insurance against the economic disabilities of failing health. It also provides inexpensive baby-tending services, as well as a pool of labor skills that may be traded informally in emergencies and part of whose value lies in the existence of a *variety* of skills.

The persistent migration to urban areas that accompanies development leads to the dispersal of nuclear families so that the extended family is attenuated and eventually disappears as members of the group find it impossible to maintain their obligations to trade informally nonmarketed services. Hence, such services have to be provided either by the market or within the *nuclear* family. To the extent that some can only be provided more cheaply within the nuclear family, this will *increase* the demand for children rather than the other way around. Not only is there an insurance motivation to maintain reasonably high parities for nuclear families, especially with respect to the provision of old-age security, but also internal baby-tending services and bases for leisure activities and affective relationships that previously were provided (cheaply) for the most part within the extended family. To some degree, higher status groups can rely more on the market, especially for servants, for

[12] Dudley Kirk, "Factors Affecting Moslem Natality," Nam, op. cit., p. 235.

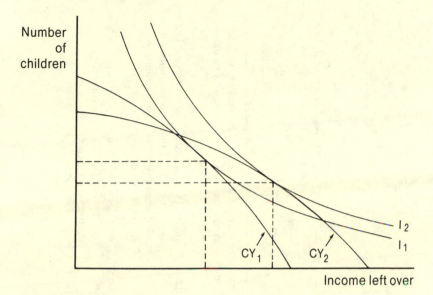

Figure 7.4

such services. The point to be stressed is that even as the extended family becomes attenuated, counteracting forces come into play that prop up the desire for fairly large (medium- to high-parity) nuclear families in the absence of economic constraints.

It would take too much space to work through all of the influences and assess what we know about these factors. Some of the major *probable* relations are suggested and summarized in table 7.2, which indicates the importance of six significant factors on the desire for medium- and high-parity children as status and per capita income increases. The table allows us to separate quickly the status-rise effects from the income-growth effects. In general, almost all of the variables work in the direction of reducing the utility of high-parity children. However, this is not the case for medium-parity children.

Both for status increases and for increases in income, there

Table 7.2

Factor	Impact of factor on desire for children as status increases		Impact of factor on desire for children as per capita income increases	
	Medium-parity children	High-parity children	Medium-parity children	High-parity children
Children as a source of:				
1. Family labor or family income	declines with status: cost offset to cost of child rearing	declines with status: cost offset to child-rearing costs	declines with income: cost offset	declines with income: cost offset
2. Old-age security	constant or increases with status	constant with status	increases as extended family declines if inadequate provision by government	decreases markedly as non-family security systems come into play
3. Extended family obligations	constant or rises with status, higher statuses frequently have greater awareness of extended family obligations	probably unimportant at high status	declines with income as extended family declines with income	of no importance as income rises

4. Insurance (against some children not capable [e.g., unemployed] or willing to contribute adequately items 1, 2, 3, or 5)	probably constant with status	probably unimportant with status	constant with income, may decline with very high increases	becomes trivial with high incomes
5. Contributions to nuclear family status maintenance and welfare	probably constant with status	probably unimportant as status rises	increases with income as extended family declines	probably unimportant
6. Impact of mortality decline effect	declines unimportant with status, son preference theory questionable	declines considerably with status	decreases as income increases	unimportant or trivial except for very rapid declines from previously very high rates

are factors that work in opposite directions in terms of their impact on the desire for medium-parity children. Especially noteworthy is what is likely to happen as per capita income increases. At least three factors are likely to stimulate an increase in the desire for children, especially as the extended family attenuates. These are the value of children (1) as a source of old-age security, (2) as a vehicle that maintains and provides nuclear family status, and (3) as a means of providing *insurance* with respect to the previously mentioned variables. On the other hand, the utility of children falls as an input that meets extended family obligations and as a contributor to family earnings. It is difficult to assess how it all nets out. It seems probable that even if on balance the desire for children does decline to some degree, the decline is not great enough to explain sufficiently the shift from a demand for almost high-parity children to low-parity children.[13]

COMBINING UTILITY AND UTILITY COST RELATIONS

On the basis of ordinary utility analysis, it follows that the utility of a marginal child, for a *given income* and *status*, falls with

[13] A theory that has to be disposed of is the idea that son preference plus declining mortality rates can explain fertility decline. The essence of the argument is that households want a target number of *surviving* sons (say, two). Because of the high mortality risk they need a higher number of male births (say, three) for two to survive, and given the sex mix that nature offers, a large family size occurs. As mortality rates decline, the risk aspect changes, and fewer male births are required. This should lead to the finding that households that have males born early (e.g., three boys out of the first three births) should have a smaller family size. Robert Repetto has marshalled as much data as he could find on the subject. He found that frequently the expected relation did not appear to hold. For instance, families whose first three births were all males had higher fertility rates than those who had only girls. The situation is more complicated. My hypothesis is that some households behave like gamblers with loaded dice. Where son preference is high, a household that finds that nature has awarded it with a string of, say, its first three conceptions that are all males, feels that nature has loaded the dice in its favor, and it keeps on playing to cash in on the winning streak. Robert Repetto, "Son Preference and Fertility Behavior in Developing Countries," *Studies in Family Planning* 4, no. 3 (April 1972): 20–76.

respect to increases in the number of children. Other things equal, utility costs are likely to rise (for given money expenditures) as we shift to higher order births. If expenditures on a fourth and fifth child are the same, then the utility cost for a fifth child will be higher than a fourth. The indirect marginal opportunity cost (say, to the mother in terms of *partial* income foregone) is likely to be approximately the same unless spacing is compressed when there are more rather than fewer births. This last is a possibility in some cases. Also, higher income foregone at slightly older ages is an additional complication. These possibilities are probably more than adequately accounted for if we assume at first that the utility costs of *higher* order births are at least the same as birth-order increases.

We can aggregate for every household the individual utility and utility cost relations. Given the jth's household income y_j, status level s_j, and the per capita income of the economy y^* to indicate the economic environment in which the household finds itself, we can determine the fertility behavior of the household.[14]

[14] In contrast to Gary Becker (see Gary Becker, "An Economic Analysis of Fertility," *Demographic and Economic Changes in Developed Countries*, National Bureau of Economic Research [Princeton: Princeton University Press, 1960], pp. 209–40), the "quality" of children is handled indirectly in this model. My theory is in the spirit of James S. Duesenberry's quip that "Economics is all about how people make choices. Sociology is all about why they don't have any choices to make." Quality is determined indirectly as a consequence of the household's reaction to its status. This seems to me to reflect more accurately what occurs in reality. I doubt whether any significant proportion of, say, middle class households consider that they have a valid option to choose between fewer children educated at their status level and *more* children nurtured and educated at a lower level.

Ultimately, this question can only be answered by empirical research. In part, it is also a scientific tactical problem that involves the determination of the optimum set of assumptions. If the quality variation *within* recognized groups is found to be exceedingly small, it might be convenient to develop the theory without the quality variable as part of the household decision making mechanism. Also, following the principle of Occam's razor, if the theory does quite well without a quality variable, it may be best to leave it out. There may be problems for which it may be useful to have quality as a household decision-making variable.

(1) $$U_{ij} = f_{ij}(y_j, s_j, y^*),$$
(2) $$U^c_{ij} = F_{ij}(y_j, s_j, y^*),$$
(3) $$y_j = fy(y^*),$$
(4) $$s_j = f_s(y^*),$$
(5) $$y^* = \text{given exogenously}$$

where U_{ij} is the utility of the ith child for the jth household and U^c_{ij} is the utility cost. Since some households move from one status to another as per capita income changes, we assume that at each level of per capita income y^* determines the status of household j. That is, y^* is a proxy for the factors that determine the distribution of occupations in the economy and the educational requirements to which the supply of labor responds.[15] With y^* given, and hence status determined, equations (1) and (2) determine the fertility behavior of the household.

As long as $U_{ij} > U_{ij}{}^c$, the household will have an incentive to have an ith child. If U_j is a monotonic-decreasing function with respect to the number of children, y^* and s_j given, then the number of births for the household is determined at the point where $U_j - U_j{}^c$ is a minimum.

We shall refer to the intersection of curves U_{ij} and U^c_{ij}, with respect to the variations in status or y^* or both, as the birth-order switch point. Up to the per capita income level (or whatever the independent variable is) of the intersection, the household is in favor of the ith birth, and beyond the switch point it is against it, or vice versa. That is, for other configurations of the two curves, the household may switch from being against

---

However, with respect to the problem at hand, my tentative approach is to have quality in terms of education, job training, and nurture enter by the back door. On this and related matters, see Harvey Leibenstein, "An Interpretation of the Economic Theory of Fertility: Promising Path or Blind Alley?" *Journal of Economic Literature,* June 1975, 457–479.

15 We could develop a more realistic looking model in which the occupation of household j depends on some previous year's per capita income, and similarly education could be a lagged function of income in the past and so on. While such a model would appear to be more realistic, it would probably add little to the essential points we are trying to make.

the ith birth to being in favor of it. More than one switch point may exist.

We should not look at the switch points as actually determining family size. For some households the switch points may be embedded within the inert areas. Thus, in some cases the number of children determined by the switch points may not generate enough pressure for the parents to do anything to prevent the switch point birth, so to speak. Hence, whether or not a switch point plays a role in determining actual family size depends on the width of the inert area bounds. Also, those in higher statuses (usually those with more education) may have narrower inert area bounds than those in lower statuses, and hence be more sensitive to the pressure generated by any particular birth. Furthermore, in the process of economic development as secular education increases, the inert areas themselves may become narrower, on the average, for all social status groups. As a result, in most groups fertility rates become more responsive to the economic forces in the environment. With these necessary background ideas in mind, we now turn to a determination of the elements that determine switch points under various circumstances.

For each status we visualize a representative household whose relations (1) and (2) are the averages of all households j. We introduce the concept of a representative household decision-making unit to simplify the exposition of the theory. Such a household would desire the average number of children of all households in the status. For the representative household j, its level of $U_{ij} = f_{ij}(y^*_k)$ is the average of the utility levels for the ith child of all households in status k, where y^*_k is the per capita income for all households in the status. We assume that y^*_k increases as y^* increases.

Consider what the utility and utility cost functions look like for the representative household in a nonextreme status.[16] We

---

[16] Extreme statuses sometimes do not follow the generalizations for nonextreme statuses. However, they are frequently unimportant numerically. For references see the citations in Freedman, op. cit.

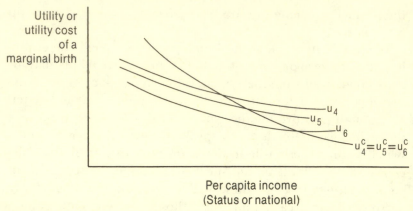

Figure 7.5

have argued that if consumption utility is constant with respect to increases in income (as per capita income increases) and the nonconsumption utilities decline slightly as income increases, then the utility function will look like the one marked u_6 in figure 7.5.

We shall begin our analysis as if there are no status-IMU goods in the utility cost functions. In that case we have argued that the actual cost is likely to be a decreasing proportion of income. Furthermore, the utility cost is likely to decline. The probable diagram for this case is illustrated in figure 7.5. Even though the utility function for children declines somewhat, it seems likely that the utility cost functions will decline more rapidly as per capita income increases. The result is increasing fertility with increases in per capita income.

The alternate situations in which the utility cost functions include status-IMU goods are illustrated in figures 7.6 and 7.7. The utility cost function presents difficulties. Status expenditures rise as income increases. However, the status expenditures may not rise sufficiently compared to the income increase to imply an increase in utility cost at the higher income. We as-

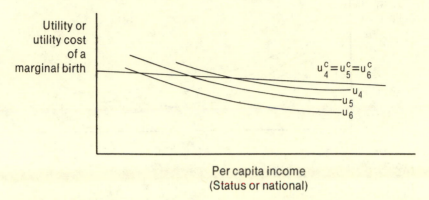

Figure 7.6

sume in figure 7.7 that the utility costs are also negatively inclined, but that they do not drop as rapidly as the utility functions. Now for each set of U_i and U_i^c (in each status) there is a "switch point" income level, up to which the household favors an ith child ($U_i > U_i^c$) and beyond which ($U_i^c > U_i$) the household is against an ith child.

The utility curves for higher parity children are drawn below each other in figure 7.6 in accordance with the arguments previously advanced. The utility cost curves probably should be drawn above each other, but the extreme case, in which the utility costs for a third, a fourth, and a fifth child are the same, simplifies the graphical analysis. If the utility cost curves cut the utility curves from below, then it is clear that the relation of the switch points to income will be such that the family size falls as income increases.

We now leave the situation of a single status and consider the economy as a whole. Once again we use the concept of the representative household, this time for the entire economy. But we keep in mind that the representative household now changes status as per capita income rises. In general, we expect that the

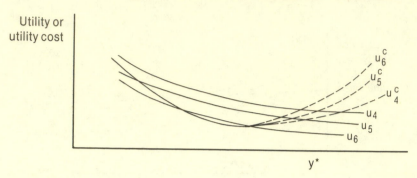

Figure 7.7

distribution of households shifts, on the average, so that smaller proportions remain in lower statuses associated with higher fertility rates, and higher proportions are in higher statuses associated with lower fertility rates. Figures 7.6 and 7.7 can be reinterpreted as representing the typical household of the economy as a whole, but we now have an additional reason for expecting to have the utility function negatively inclined. Also, the *status-shift* effect should result in the utility cost function to be positively inclined or less negatively inclined.

A final possibility worth considering is the one in which the utility cost function first declines and then rises with increases in per capita income. In the illustration in figure 7.7 the U-shaped utility cost curve at first cuts the utility curves from above. If we examine the birth-order switch points, we see that this involves a situation in which the initial consequence of development (per capita income increase) is an increase in fertility, but this trend eventually reverses itself and shifts to a sustained decline in fertility.

The possibility shown in figure 7.7 is that the status-IMU-goods hump, so to speak, becomes relatively more important as we move towards higher parity children. In other words, higher parity children require that the household give up some of its status goods, and furthermore, in accordance with our previous analysis, this possibility may increase with income. This is illustrated in figure 7.7 by the broken lines that reflect higher parity utility costs. It is possible that considerations of this kind may have led to the very rapid drop in fertility in a country such as Japan during the postwar period.

We have shown that the use of utility cost curves that are functions of status and income will, in general (but not invariably), lead to patterns of immediate or eventual sustained fertility decline as a consequence of development. It is to be noted that the assumptions behind the theory do not have built into them sufficient and necessary conditions for fertility decline. But the arguments presented suggest that the parameters of the functions, taking status-IMU goods into account, are probably such as to be consistent with fertility decline in the course of economic development. We cannot prove that fertility must decline as per capita income increases in the course of economic development. But adding the status-IMU goods variable to other elements that work in the direction of fertility decline buttresses the arguments that exist and increases our capacity to explain fertility decline in the course of economic development. The inert area part of the theory in which this analysis is embedded enables us to explain the frequently observed fact that actual fertility in many households may be greater than desired at many junctures in the development process.

8 | Who Does What: Organizations and Environments

INTRODUCTION

By "who" we have in mind types of enterprises and environments, and not specific individuals. Conventional microeconomic theory does not consider the relevance of "who does what" in terms of the type of enterprise or organization that carries out economic activities. Does it matter if economic activities are carried out by family farms, urban family enterprises, large private enterprises, small public enterprises, cooperatives, ministries of production, etc.?

A basic question rarely considered by development economists deals with the relationship between the organizational structure of the economy and the motivating factors that influence organizational behavior. This, of course, is very much connected with the question as to how well economic plans of any sort, at the micro or macro level, can be implemented. The essential question is how well the economic units or economic organisms carry out the expected economic activities. While in general we should concern ourselves with both consumption and production units, our focus here is on production activities. To see what is involved it may be useful to go back to the list of elements considered in chapter two. These were such entities as the basic decision units, the concept of effort, the inert area idea, the agent-principal relations, the significance of interpersonal interactions, and the significance of individual motivation as an input. Our basic thesis is that a given organization with given resources can lead to wide variations in productivity.

The thinking behind our basic analytical approach, which determines how well an organization carries out its economic activities, can be summarized by the following set of propositions: (1) the results of organizational behavior depend on the behavior of its individual members; (2) the individual members are primarily agents of the true principals, and as agents they may pursue objectives which are different from those of their principals; (3) the agents' contracts are in general incomplete; (4) individual performance depends on the specific effort choices of the individuals involved; (5) because of contract incompleteness, effort is to a considerable degree a discretionary variable; (6) within the discretionary bounds the effort choices depend on the motivating factors which influence individual behavior; (7) these motivating forces can be strong or weak or distortional, depending on the nature of the organization, and apart from the resources available to it; (8) these motivating forces will in part depend on the interplay between the internal motivations and its external environment; e.g., the environment may be competitive or noncompetitive; (9) as a result of the above considerations, we can see that organizations with the same resources but with a different history or motivating context may show very different results with respect to output.

The significance of the above considerations can be seen in a number of areas. For example, analyses which depend on different capital output ratios should take into account that output for given amounts of capital may differ markedly, depending on organizational considerations. By the same token the rate of development will depend only partially on the rate of investment or the allocation of resources for growth. Obviously, growth rates will also be determined by these organizational-motivational elements. Clearly the related area of development planning, if it is to be realistic, must take into account the general X-inefficiency considerations implicit in the elements considered in the previous paragraph. To the extent that such plans depend, directly or indirectly, on input-output ratios they must implicitly depend on motivational and organizational considerations.

No attempt will be made to examine the implications of all the alternative ways of organizing economic activities. Rather, an attempt will be made to indicate the relevance of general X-efficiency theory to a particular type of economic entity—the state enterprise. We shall focus our attention on some of the ways in which X-inefficiency can enter state run enterprises—enterprises in which governments are the main or only stockholders. Such firms are usually run by appointed managers and not directly by ministries or government departments. Such enterprises, outside of countries run by communist governments, are a growing phenomenon. In the analysis which follows we shall not be concerned with the political issues surrounding such enterprises or with the political or social reasons for their being. We shall dwell on the economic aspects of the problem and shall remark only briefly on the relation between ideology and efficiency.

A great many considerations enter the evaluation of state enterprises. Among these are questions regarding the market structure, the relation to government, the relation to equity, the connection between economic and imposed social functions of such enterprises, the elements that constitute market of profit criteria for operation, etc. All of these considerations influence efficiency. However, our analysis will focus only on X-efficiency aspects.

There is considerable analysis in the general economics literature with respect to the notion that governmental interferences with private enterprises do not lead to allocative efficiency, since such interferences distort the prices upon which economic decisions are made. Subsidies, taxes, or other controls that result in deviations from free market equilibrium prices must result in decisions that misallocate resources. We shall not examine this question. Our view is that even if prices are "right," so to speak, the inputs may still be used ineffectively. Our view will be that we have to examine the nature of the economic organization, *and the environment* in which it operates, to determine to what extent X-inefficiency exists under the circumstances in question.

At the outset we have to clarify the relation between X-efficiency and allocative efficiency, at least in one respect— namely, that in an important sense allocative efficiency depends on X-efficiency, and not the other way round. When analyzing the relation between X-efficiency and allocative efficiency, we have to separate the demand for *factors* of production in the marketplace from the utilization of these factors in terms of effort inputs. Hence, we shall adopt a convention so that when we speak about market supply and demand for factors, we shall use the word "factors," and, when we are concerned with X-efficiency, we shall use the concept of effort input. For a given output the greater the effort input the less the demand of specific factors in the marketplace, assuming the demand for the goods into which the inputs go are given. Equilibrium prices of factors depend on the productivity of factors, which is to say that they depend on how effectively inputs are used; that is, on the degree of X-inefficiency of effort input use in firms. Conventional theory implicitly assumes that the degree of X-efficiency is given. Of course, in our view it is a variable. But for purposes of our analysis it is important *not* to assume that everything is in some grand general equilibrium so that the analysis can be carried out.

It is clear that X-inefficiency within all firms will determine the demand for factors, and, for intermediate goods, X-inefficiency elements will also determine the supply of factors. Even if a given factor market approximates an equilibrium price, the input in question may be used in a variety of industries, some of which may be closer to competitive industries, while others may be monopolies or oligopolies. It is quite possible that the monopolies will use the effort inputs much less effectively than the competitive industries. In any event, whatever the equilibrium price in the factor market and whatever the *average* degree of effort input utilization, there may be great deviations in utilization in specific instances compared to either the average degree of utilization or optimal degree of utilization.

In general, we should expect that the price of any specific factor which yields effort inputs will depend on the effort choices made and hence on the way in which these choices influence the demand and supply of the factors of production. In the analysis that follows, we shall be more concerned with the specific problem of input utilization for specific firms and with the consequences for determining the cost of production, rather than with the general problem of determining the demand and supply of factors of production in the marketplace.

The basic approach which we shall spell out in the ensuing sections is that the nature of the organization carrying out economic activities and the environment in which it is imbedded will generate two opposing sets of forces: one of these leads to a tendency towards high costs (or towards increasing costs), while the other generates *cost containing* (or cost decreasing) influences. The struggle between these two sets of factors will determine actual costs. In section three we explain briefly this general viewpoint, while in section four we apply it to the problem of X-inefficiency in state-owned enterprises. But first some remarks about the relation between ideology and efficiency may be appropriate, since the operations of state enterprises are also likely to involve ideological considerations.

IDEOLOGY AND X-EFFICIENCY

We consider first the relations between some basic beliefs about the economy and X-efficiency. These general belief systems are extremely important because they involve visions as to how the economy works and therefore influence the nature of the enterprises that are set up. While we are not concerned with political ideologies as such, we should be concerned with the relationship between ideology and efficiency, and especially with the consequences of ideological considerations when such considerations are put into practice. We cannot examine all possible ideological positions; however, by looking at three positions, we can indicate the general nature of the argument and its relation to general X-efficiency theory.

We will begin with the neoclassical system. While the neoclassical system is not, strictly speaking, an ideology (it is a scheme of economic analysis), it may be looked at as an ideology, since prescriptions based on that system are sometimes advocated without a close examination of the underlying assumptions involved. According to the strict neoclassical viewpoint, there is no relation between the formal controller of the firm and the behavior of the firm. Thus a one man firm, or a family enterprise, or a large corporation whose stock is widely distributed, or a firm whose stock is owned by the government are all presumed to operate the same way. Usually this is an implicit rather than an explicit presumption of the theory. In most textbook expositions the question is not really raised. Nevertheless the view that firms maximize profits and minimize costs, irrespective of who owns them, ignores or really assumes away the basic X-efficiency questions. Obviously the view we take is that it makes a considerable difference whether those who control the firm are motivated either in terms of personality or context to struggle against the cost raising influences that exist. Furthermore, we shall see that the separation between the responsibility for certain activities and the rewards associated with responsibilities can lead to a type of buck-passing phenomenon which generates costs considerably above minimum costs. In fact, it will turn out that this will be the general view to be taken with respect to various belief systems. In other words, the difficulty with most belief systems is that they assume, albeit unthinkingly, that enterprises naturally attempt to minimize costs. The main message of X-efficiency theory is that this is not at all a natural phenomenon; nor are profits a good index of efficiency; a given rate of profit may be consistent with low costs and low prices or a manipulated context which results in higher costs and higher prices.

A second ideological view may be called the anticapitalist argument. The crux of this argument is that exploitation is in some sense measured by profits and that profits are evil. Hence profits have to be kept to very low levels or eliminated. At first blush this argument seems to be the exact opposite of the neoclassical argument, but in fact it turns out to be very similar. The argument focuses on profit levels as the criterion for the "rightness" of the operation of the enterprise. Somehow if profits can be kept at the "right size" all is well. The important thing, of course, is that in focusing on profits those who espouse this view are looking at the wrong dial. It is as if we attempted to judge the efficiency of an automobile by looking at the temperature gauge. There are three basic considerations when examining the efficiency of an operation, and looking at only two of them can be misleading. The three considerations are profits, prices, and costs. Costs and profits per unit may determine prices, but looking only at profits does not tell us whether prices are high or low. Profits may be low, zero, or even negative, and at the same time production may be carried on at such a degree of X-inefficiency that prices are very much higher than necessary.

Another approach that at first appears to be the exact opposite of the anticapitalist ideology leads to the same result. This is the one that looks at profits as the measure of efficiency—the higher the profits the more efficient. In this case high profits are usually deemed to be good, while in the anticapitalist ideology they are bad—but the gauge we are focusing on is the same. This is not to suggest that under this approach higher profits are always looked upon as more desirable than somewhat lower profits, but in general "profitable operations" are used as a guide for the appropriate operation of the enterprise. Once again the price variable and its relation to cost are not examined. Clearly, where the enterprise operates in a monopolistic or cartel-like environment, it is conceivable for prices to be sufficiently high to allow simultaneously a reasonable level of profits and relatively high costs compared to minimum costs. We need not go into all the possibilities here. Some of these have already been considered above. It suffices to say that the ideologies considered for the operation of enterprises which are either subject to public control or to public concern are really not appropriate because they do not take into account the possible degrees of X-inefficiency permitted by their organizational structure and by the environment in which they are imbedded. Of special concern in some cases are the qualitative aspects of the commodity or service involved. Where these are sold directly to consumers, an apparently low price may in fact not be low at all when the quality aspects are taken into account.

EFFORT, RESPONSIBILITY, AND COST CONSEQUENCES

In order to analyze how well an organization uses the factors of production, we have to examine the relation between the "impactors" and the "impactees" of effort discretion. To see what is involved, consider two extreme cases. On the one extreme we will be concerned with complete individual responsibility; on the other, complete individual irresponsibility.

Now, consider the case in which every firm is a one-man firm. That is, the entrepreneur, manager, and worker are all the same individual. All trades take place in the marketplace. Every individual is under these circumstances completely responsible for the consequences of his effort. If his effort is less, he has less of value to offer in the market, and he receives less in return. The main point, and it is one that cannot be overemphasized, is that there are no losses, as a consequence of an individual ac-tion, that are or can be imposed on others. This is basically the case that fits best the neoclassical microtheory.

Now let us consider the other extreme, the complete irresponsibility case. All firm members are hired on a time basis, but they are not responsible directly to the "stockholders." There may be either a very wide distribution of shareholders or, in the case of publicly run corporations, the shareholders or principals are ultimately the citizens at large. Each person is hired on the basis of time, and there is considerable effort discretion. Now, if an individual were asked whether he would like rules under which he is responsible for the consequences of his activities or rules under which he is not responsible, he would almost invariably choose the latter. As a result, activities (or effort positions, or parts of effort positions) which impose costs on the organization are simply passed on to others. That is, the costs are not borne in any way by the individuals who use their discretionary powers to carry out the activities they choose to carry out. Also, the consequences of activities by one individual can, in a variety of ways, be passed on to still other individuals and ultimately either to the stockholders or to consumers. In other words, it is possible for all *intermediate impactees* to pass on the consequences of activities to others outside the organization. It may be useful to consider that the critical element here is whether or not the "effort-responsibility-consequences" connection (ERC) is kept within the appropriate decision-making unit. The enterprise may be viewed as a hierarchical collection of such decision-making units starting with the individual and shifting towards larger, more encompassing collections of individuals, until the entire firm is included. If the ERCs are kept within the individual then of course the individual is completely responsible for the results of his activities. But if the ERC relations go beyond the individual, the responsibility-consequences connection may or may not be contained within some sufficiently small decision-making unit that can react to and correct for the consequences. For analytical purposes it is clearly important to determine how far responsibility is shifted—to what extent the ERCs are kept within large decision-making bounds, or to what extent they go beyond the bounds of the enterprise itself. In the case of monopolies under which internal (but not strictly necessary) costs can be added to the price, the ultimate burden is shifted to consumers. In this particular case the ERCs are not kept within the bounds of the enterprise as a decision-making unit. While actual situations are in between the two extremes of complete individual responsibility and of complete irresponsibility, it is important to keep the extreme irresponsibility picture in mind in order to see that the analysis of the locus of responsibility within an organization and its environment can help us to determine how such organizations influence the rate of development. Clearly irresponsibility increases costs of production. Furthermore, costs are important in determining the rate of development. In fact, high enough costs of production can nullify the value of new investment. There is no point in producing things, in the country in question, with new equipment, if the products can be imported more cheaply from abroad, or if they can be produced more cheaply with the old equipment. Obviously new investment makes economic sense only if goods can be produced more cheaply than would be the case without the new investment. The nature of the productive organization under which new economic activities are to take place can frequently result in cost increases so that anticipated improvements do not occur.

In figure 8.1 we indicate diagrammatically the nature of the ideas we have just discussed. We assume that an individual constraint concern will depend in part on the nature of his socialization, but in part on the effort of others. Hence the degree of pressure which reflects the efforts of authorities, as well as of peer groups, will help determine the exact point of performance that an individual will undertake. If pressure is less then constraint concern is less, and performance will be lower. In the illustration it will never drop to zero because of the stand-

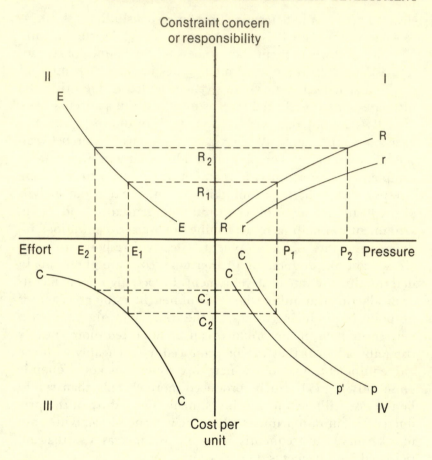

Figure 8.1

ards an individual brings from the outside to the job. These pressures not only determine performance in the sense of the activities that an individual will carry out, but also include activities which attempt to impose internal responsibility for higher costs, as against those which result in shifts to ultimate impactees outside the firm. Thus, when we examine the possible X-inefficiency aspects of state-run enterprises, we should keep in mind that the result will depend on the way in which the organization imposes pressures on individuals, which in itself then determines individual degrees of constraint concern.

In quadrant one of figure 8.1 the curve marked RR relates pressure "by the firm" on the individual to the degree of constraint concern (i.e., responsibility) he will assume in response to pressure. Pressure is the independent variable, constraint concern the dependent variable. In quadrant two the curve EE relates constraint concern to effort put forth; constraint concern is now the independent variable and effort the dependent variable. In quadrant three the curve CC relates effort to that part of cost of production per unit contributed by the individual. In this case a higher degree of effort is associated with the lower cost and vice versa. Finally, in quadrant four cost is the independent variable, which in turn determines the pressure that the firm will put forth on the individual. We note that as the curves are drawn there is one set of values that is consistent with the others, i.e., equilibrium values. This is the set of values represented by the point $P_1R_1E_1C_2$. In this case all the values for pressure, constraint concern, effort, and cost of production are consistent with each other. Should this point occur no change would take place. We note that the "outside cobweb" indicated by the "point" $P_2R_2E_2C_1$ are not consistent with each other and lead in a cobweb fashion to narrower circles approaching the equilibrium values $P_1R_1E_1C_2$. We should expect, because of the theory of inert areas, that the equilibrium point will not be unique. Rather, we should expect the existence of an equilibrium set of points containing the point $P_1R_1E_1C_2$. In general, we see that the basic relation is the curve RR. This reflects the extent to which the environment puts pressure on the firm, which in turn puts pressure on the individual. Thus, if RR were lower as illustrated by the curve rr, this would reflect less pressure and ultimately a still higher equilibrium cost of production.

We can readily see that the equilibrium will be determined

by the extent to which the cost-pressure relationship CP moves to the left (say to CP'), i.e., toward less pressure for each cost level. Thus, in the extreme case in which everyone shifts cost to others and in which costs are ultimately shifted outside of the firm, the extent of the costs imposed will depend on the degree to which CP' is to the left of the original value CP; the further CP' is to the left of CP the higher the level of equilibrium costs. This is not to say that there are no cost containing influences. However, the lesser the extent of such influences the greater the curve CP' is to the left of CP.

An issue which arises is whether the curve RR in quadrant one shifts towards the abscissa, say to rr. In other words, as the degree of responsibility is generally reduced, is the constraint concern reaction lessened for a given degree of imposed pressure? It would seem reasonable to assume that to some degree this is likely to be the case. Thus, movements which involve organizational entropy will usually be depicted by the CP curve's moving to the left and the rr curve's moving towards the abscissa. Whether or not the curve rr moves is not really important, since the entire analysis can be carried as a consequence of movements of the curve CP to CP'. However, for purposes of generality, it would seem useful to include the possibility that the curve rr may also move towards the abscissa.

The next set of considerations involves the cost containing influences. Despite the fact that costs are shifted ultimately outside the firm, they do not move necessarily to infinite levels. We can list four elements which are likely to operate as cost-containing factors. These are (1) standards of performance, (2) the maximum revenue available to the organization, (3) the degree of competition, and/or (4) the degree of bureaucratic control. We have already discussed standards of performance; presumably there will always be some minimal standard of performance so that there is a maximum degree of cost per unit, even if no other controls are operative. Since the other cost-containing elements are likely to be more important on the imposition of external pressure than standards of performance, it is not necessary to defend the previous proposition. If the revenue of an organization depends on the sale of commodities, then obviously there is a maximum revenue which is likely to exist. Where the elasticity of demand is inversely related to price, gross revenue is likely to be largest at the point where the demand function approximates unity.

Although governments or other organizations are likely to add to the revenues out of tax receipts to make up for losses by the organization (e.g., the Post Office), there may be such a thing as a maximal budget subsidy. This operates as a second or third level of cost control. More important than either of these, (maximal revenue and maximal subsidy) is likely to be the "tightness of the environment." This may depend on the degree of competition either outside or within the country. Such competition may exist because of the possibility of importing substitutes as well as shifting to substitutes within the economy. Clearly the closeness of substitutes and the related extent and sense of competition can become a significant cost containing influence.

Finally, a highly variable influence is the degree of bureaucratic control of the organization at a higher level than the producing organization. The influence of this variable clearly depends on the nature of the control and the motivation of those in higher levels of authority. Nevertheless, all of these four cost-containing factors can lead to results which are significant above minimal costs. This is illustrated in figure 8.2. The lowest curve associated with the degree of environmental tightness becomes the operative cost-containing influence. There is a variety of means in which the tightness of cost control can manifest itself, and we have already mentioned four of these. Degree of competition probably represents the simplest example of an environmental cost-containing force. The four curves marked *S, R, B,* and *C* represent respectively standards of performance (*S*), *maximum revenue* (*R*), bureaucratic control (*B*), and com-

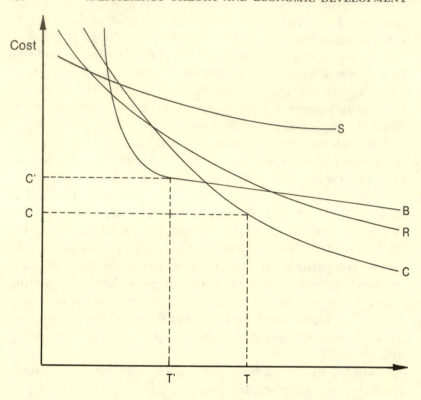

Degree of "environmental tightness"

Figure 8.2

petition (*C*), as a means of control. For any degree of tightness the level of costs will be determined by the *lowest* cost containment curve associated with the degree of environmental control. Thus in the diagram at the point *T* the competition curve is the lowest cost containment curve, and hence this becomes the operative control. If competition were absent then the operative control at *T* would be the level of bureaucratic control as indicated in the diagram. Of course, without competition, the level of bureaucratic control might involve a lesser degree of tightness, and hence the curve T would shift to the left, to, let us say, T'.

In any event, the same principle follows in that the lowest curve determines the operative control, and by the same token higher curves are at that point inoperative.

COMMENTS ON X-EFFICIENCY IN STATE ENTERPRISES

The comments in this section are mostly of a general nature, although some of them are suggested by the experience of specific enterprises in Bolivia and Indonesia which have been studied in some detail by Malcolm Gillis. A number of other investigators are mentioned as a basis for the Gillis[1] study, and hence indirectly they may also form a basis for these comments. Thus what follows is only in part theoretical. Part depends on actual observations and empirical reports on state enterprises in two developing countries.

Because of the history of how public enterprises arise, or because of ideological considerations, public enterprises are likely to be sheltered from competitive pressures. Consider two possible historical aspects. In many cases the enterprise was originally a private firm. However, as a consequence of its failure as a private firm, it was taken over by the government. The alternative case is that the private company is taken over for ideological reasons, irrespective of its failure or success as a private firm. In either case the government has an incentive to minimize competitive pressures, the manager of the firm has the same incentive, and when the two cooperate they are in a good position to achieve their joint aims. This is not to argue that a

---

[1] This section is based largely on an excellent essay by Malcolm Gillis, "Allocative Efficiency and X-Efficiency in State Owned Enterprises: Some Asian and Latin American Cases in the Mining Sector," Unpublished (May 1977). Copies are available from Mr. Gillis, Harvard Institute of International Development, Harvard University, Cambridge, Mass.

monopoly necessarily emerges. For one thing there may be foreign competition that cannot be eliminated. For another, there may exist islands of private enterprise that persist and compete. We can hardly generalize on the vast array of possible potential configurations. There is no question about the tendency toward monopoly in government run enterprises. Of course, a lack of competition makes it easier for the state enterprise to be profitable, to appear to be operating successfully according to commercial principle, and in this manner to make no claims on the state budget.

There is one special consideration as to why we should expect public enterprises to be less X-efficient in general than private enterprises. The natural selection argument for efficiency in private enterprise is usually not operative in the public sector. To be brief, public enterprises are usually not allowed to die. In addition, there is usually no entry into this sector to provide substitutes. Of prime importance is the fact that very high costs in public enterprises do not operate as an incentive for entry of lower cost organizations. As a consequence, losses and bankruptcies do not lead to a situation in which only the somewhat more efficient enterprises survive, or more efficient organizations enter. As a result, even higher X-inefficient enterprises may continue to survive at public expense, since relatively few pressures are available to alter the situation. This is especially likely to be the case where the public enterprises are also expected to carry out noneconomic functions, or, as they are usually phrased—social functions. This is not to say that extreme inefficiency and extreme losses do not in some cases set in motion bureaucratic and political activities which attempt to reduce excessive costs to some degree, but the system is not set up in such a way so that one could count on such countervailing influences taking place—even with reasonable length lags. As a result, built-in X-inefficiency of various types is to be expected in the operation of public enterprises.

Of equal or greater importance than the question of the containment of day to day costs is the problem of introducing improvements and innovations. The same notions apply. The incentives to introduce innovations in private enterprises are either not operative, or not operative to the same degree for reasons already suggested. In addition, the civil-service atmosphere surrounding executives in public enterprises leads to a situation under which they are likely to be risk-averse with respect to the adoption of innovations.

While there is a wide variety of rules which encumber decision making in public enterprises, X-inefficiency can be caused by rules which are overly circumscribed, as well as by rules that are too loose. In general, there will be a tendency for close circumscription of activities. This is almost a natural result in organizations closely tied to civil service or closely tied to a civil-service image. The net result is the production of goods according to rules rather than according to an individual sense of responsibility for production. In a sense, almost anything that does not fit the rules simply is not carried-out. Since the rules are rarely set up to fit the nature of the organization and the activities suitable for the organization, it is generally the case that closely circumscribed rules lead to inadequate responsibility and relatively high costs.

The other extreme which is likely to exist for enterprises that are in the early stages of their inception, or of their being taken over by the state, is too much latitude. This leads to a situation in which the enterprise is operated primarily for the benefit of groups close to the enterprise, rather than in the service of consumers. Once again, this is almost a natural outcome, especially in situations where there is no clear-cut connection between the rewards for the activities of the enterprise and service to consumers. This is the case where the enterprises are monopolies. Thus, even if managers are expected to operate *profitable* enterprises, these need not serve consumers. As monopolies they could pass on inefficiencies in terms of higher costs and still be profitable. At the same time these higher costs may be an expression of or consequences of serving groups which are in some sense close to the enterprise. Such groups may be those who are the managers, or close to the managers, or those with sufficient political influence, so that some degree of cooperation has to exist between the manager and the politicians or the government appointees involved.

Finally, the case under which there exists a multiplicity of functions for the enterprise, including "social functions," is likely to create a situation in which high costs are used as a rationalization for high X-inefficiencies. In other words, it is rare that the costs of these social functions are determined in advance and separated from the purely economic activities, so that the commercial viability of the enterprise can be judged apart from the costs of the social functions. There are two problems involved here: one is whether the social functions are of a type so that the costs of carrying out these functions can be separated from the purely economic activities of the enterprise. This is a question of the possibility of accountability for social functions. The second problem is that even if accountability for the social functions is possible, there will frequently be no attempt made to account separately for the social and economic activities of the enterprise.

There are a number of cases in the literature in which firms do not introduce improvements when it is profitable to do so and when there is no conflict with profitability or with proposed social objectives.[2] There is a variety of reasons why this should take place. Two of the more important ones have to do with tradition in the enterprise of an inert area type. That is, the arguments against innovation take the form of "we have always done things this way" or "things are not usually done this way." Such traditions are usually very strong. Traditions are likely to manifest themselves in particular rules of behavior or apparently sanctified procedures. In their turn such sanctified proce-

2 See Harvey Leibenstein, *Beyond Economic Man* (Cambridge, Mass.: Harvard University Press, 1976), pp. 29–34, 42–44. See also Gillis, op. cit.

dures support tradition. It is usually not sufficient for "things not to be done this way." It obviously helps the maintenance of the tradition if things are usually done in some other way. This is not to argue that traditions are never broken, or that at times there is not a bias for novelty, if even for its own sake, but only that the fact that to most actors the burden of proof will be on the new approach may be sufficient reason to give a strong and continuing advantage to traditional procedures. Since the incentives for changing traditional activities are likely to be weak, innovations are not introduced. In fact, frequently there is simply no penalty to members of the organization or even top management for *not* introducing improvements when it is profitable to do so.

A significant distinction must be made between what is rational from the viewpoint of the power structure and what is rational from the viewpoint of efficiency. Power has a rationality and reward system of its own. The hierarchical structure that supports specialization also supports power. One of the presumed advantages of power is that you do not necessarily have to listen to those below you. In fact, the scarcity of time at the top almost requires that those at the highest levels find means of restricting access to the top.

Thus the managements of public enterprises are likely to possess non-optimal internal information flow systems so that, even though the possibility of an improvement might be clearly known somewhere in the organization, there is no way of getting the appropriate information to the attention of individuals who may be either capable or interested in instituting the profitable changes. Finally, there is frequently a division between those capable of introducing changes as against those who might be interested in doing so. In other words, the nature of public enterprises in the absence of competition does not lead to organizational structures which evolve so that appropriate changes are frequently introduced. On evolutionary grounds one could argue that under competition organizational structures that make it difficult to introduce changes cannot persist. They will be forced out in competition with superior organizational structures. This is not to argue that the evolutionary argument is so forceful, even under a private enterprise system, that the most efficient *always* survive. Rather, the argument is more modest. We intend to suggest nothing more than that in the two cases, competitive enterprise versus public enterprise, the latter is likely to be consistent with organizational structures under which it is difficult to introduce improvements and there is little to prevent such organizational structures from surviving for long periods of time.

The Gillis studies referred to earlier contain a number of examples of firms in which opportunities for gain were not taken advantage of. Three mining enterprises, one in Bolivia and two in Indonesia, referred to as *A, B,* and *C,* were isolated for special analysis. In one case, enterprise *B,* a change in the law made it profitable to mine tin of a relatively low-grade and to send the tin to a central point for upgrading, rather than to try to mine only high-quality ore. This would have increased profits by $2 million. The possibility of doing so was known from 1966, but the practice itself was not changed for six years—until 1972. In another case, firm *C,* mining activities, which included simultaneously the mining of precious metals, were abandoned even though technologists employed by the company knew of profitable techniques to exploit the veins of precious metals. Nevertheless, this was not done, most likely because of communication blockages between the high-level technicians in the firm who had the necessary information and those in a position to make decisions.

Inefficient internal communication systems were also responsible for other X-inefficiencies in state-run enterprises. In the Indonesian firms studied, bureaucratic controls required a large number of accounting reports to be filed. Managers complained that they were overwhelmed by a sea of numbers. But they were inappropriate numbers. At the same time, the information that would have been useful for managerial decision making was not, in fact, collected. For example, inventory control problems were particularly serious. The accounting department was reported to make little use of the detailed information developed by the inventory section, although both departments were in the same building.

The organizational structure and the personnel problems of the firms analyzed also created X-inefficiency. For example, the authority of managers was unclear. All the mines reported to a technical director in the capital city. As a consequence, the chief technical engineer had a span of control so excessively wide that effective control was impossible. At the same time, seniority provisions put older engineers with little recent technical information in important positions, whereas younger engineers with newer information found it very difficult to get into positions in which information could flow from them to higher levels of decision making.

A particularly interesting case had to do with rotation policies at mine sites. Managers would spend a short period in a specific mine and, in order to make a good record, would carry out what was referred to as the "cream skimming of deposits." While this might help the record of the existing manager, it made it difficult for subsequent managers. This practice was not in the interest of long-run maximizing profits—i.e., short-run considerations took precedence over long-run rationale.

Finally, it is worth noting that the environment in which these organizations operated had a strong built-in bias against innovations. If profits were adequate, the innovations would lead to very little gain, if any, for the manager who was employed, more or less, on a civil-service basis. In other words, the manager did not share in the higher profit or higher production attributable to the innovation. On the other hand, if the innovation turned into a loss, the manager was then in an adverse position. Losses attributable to an innovation were readily noticed, and the manager involved would face difficulties in the civil-service promotion system. As a result, the manager had a strong incentive to leave well enough alone.

All of the matters previously discussed were additionally complicated by the introduction of social goals. These frequently degenerated into vague assertions about how society was served or, more likely, they were used to rationalize inept performances. Needless to say, this decreased the ability of the system to determine accountability in accordance with results. While, on the whole, we have emphasized the likely negative possibilities of the operation of public enterprises, the arguments presented support the general theory that "who does what" matters and, that in the interest of high levels of X-efficiency, the authorities in developing countries ought to be concerned with the questions of who ought to do what and under what system of organizational incentives.

GENERAL X-EFFICIENCY ANALYSIS
AND ORGANIZATION—THE WIDER PICTURE

The organizational arrangements within an economy determine the degree of X-efficiency in the economy. The basic underlying approach of this chapter is that the motivational aspects inherent in economic organizations can be studied. We suggested the nature of the motivational analysis of productive units by focusing attention on the case of state enterprises, and especially on those state enterprises which operated as monopolies. But we only skimmed the surface of our enquiries, in part, because this is a topic which has not been well developed by economists. If all state enterprises are the same, we are likely to get one result, but if they differ a much more complex analysis is required. However, the ideas applied to state enterprises can also be applied to other types of productive organizations ranging from small strictly private enterprises within a competitive environment to large monopolistic private enterprises, and finally to the production activities of government bureaucracies themselves.

To close this chapter it may be useful to summarize the basic ideas we have employed and at the same time suggest the wider applicability of the approach. In essence we are concerned with three types of pressures which influence X-efficiency. These are the pressures which stem from (1) the environment in which the organization is located, (2) the internal structure of the organization, and (3) the traditional procedures that exist in the organization which in turn are a consequence of its history. The environmental pressures determine whether or not the productive results of the effort choices of organization members are checked in any way—either by competition within the environment or by other monitoring devices within the organizational system. Competition may be viewed as a relatively effective and inexpensive monitoring device of a special type.

The internal structure is much more complex to analyze and depends in general on the relationship between responsibility, the reward system, and the possibilities of shifting responsibility and the consequences of irresponsibility to others—and eventually outside of the organization itself. More on this below. The traditional influences are likely to determine to what extent traditional procedures inhibit undertakings or use more effective procedures which may not be sanctioned by tradition.

The essential element of our analytical scheme depends on an examination of the extent to which individuals are really responsible for the productive results of their activities. According to the neoclassical view, individuals are supposed to be paid a reward (wage, or profit, etc.) equal to the monetary value of their marginal *productivity*. But this is the result in an *ideal* case. It is the situation that comes about when firms *minimize* costs, which is to say when X-inefficiency is equal to zero. But of course this is exactly the special case we are not interested in. In fact this approach to the problem may be said to close analytical doors. We have tried to show through general X-efficiency analysis how to open such analytical doors. Hence we have argued that in circumstances under which production is not exceptionally tightly monitored (the normal case) organization members will have an incentive to reduce accountability for their productivity. In fact, if payment is separated from productivity, as it is frequently, then many individuals will want to minimize responsibility for their actions, which will usually separate productivity accounting from their effort choices. As each individual tries to shift his responsibility away from himself, the consequences of such shifts will, directly or indirectly, fall on others. Furthermore, in the case of monopoly or a weakly monitored environment, there is the capacity to shift responsibility-consequences ultimately onto consumers, by the device of raising prices inversely to the degree to which effort responsibility is shifted outside the enterprise. Hence the essential aspect of the internal motivational analysis is to see to what extent the reward system and the system of interpersonal relations allow considerable shifts in the effort-responsibility-consequences connections beyond the decision-making unit, or to what extent there are constraining influences that keep these connections with the appropriate decision-making units.

Index